Family
Foundations

Family Foundations

Four Stories of
Black Washtenaw County
Community Building,
1850 to 1950

Fifth Avenue Press is a locally focused and publicly owned publishing imprint of the Ann Arbor District Library. It is dedicated to supporting the local writing community by promoting the production of original fiction, nonfiction, and poetry written for children, teens, and adults.

Printed in the United States of America

First Printing 2024

Layout and Illustration: Ann Arbor District Library

ISBN: 978-1-956697-43-8 (Paperback)

Fifth Avenue Press
343 S. Fifth Ave
Ann Arbor, MI 48104
fifthavenue.press

CONTENTS

Foreword

I WAS DEEPLY HONORED TO BE ASKED to contribute a foreword to this important, dynamic, two-century history of African-American families and communities in Ypsilanti and Ann Arbor. The histories of the Asher Aray, Bass, Jewett, and Kersey families recounted in this volume—and the accompanying African American Cultural and Historical Museum of Washtenaw County (AACHM)[1] exhibition—do so much more than take us back to the earliest decades and to the Black families who settled here. By taking the reader on these families' journeys across the 19th and 20th centuries and up to the present, *Family Foundations* documents the love, community support, and resiliency that has sustained these families through national and local landscapes deeply resistant to racial progress even in the best of times. To quote Bryan Stevenson of the Equal Justice Initiative: "To overcome racial inequality, we must confront our history."[2] This is what makes *Family Foundations* such an important contribution to the history of Washtenaw County.

Family Foundations is exemplary of the many contributions to the social and cultural life of Washtenaw County that the AACHM has made during the more than three decades that the museum has been devoted to the mission of compiling and telling the histories of Black communities and families in the county. From the Underground Railroad Tour to the Living Oral History project, the museum's many traveling and online exhibits, and now with the museum itself at 1528 Pontiac Trail, the AACHM has remade the work of local history in our communities into one which reflects the true multiracial and multicultural character of our communities.

I first came to know the museum when I was asked as a young University of Michigan (U-M) history professor to contribute, in my own small way, to the collaborative research that would come to form the basis of the Underground Railroad Tour. More recently, it has been my privilege to be a member of the team of local historians, community activists, U-M professors and students—anchored by members of the AACHM—who formed the Black Washtenaw Collaboratory (BWC),[3] whose mission is to build on the histories of African-American community building in Washtenaw County and to place those histories in the context of a community that, for more than a century, has continually adopted policies and practices designed to maintain racial segregation and inequality.

Ann Arbor has been my home for thirty years. I want to share with you a little of my story of moving to Ann Arbor in order to make it clear why I think the *Family Foundations* project is so important to establish racial justice in our community. When my wife and I first moved to Ann Arbor in the early 1990s, we lived on North Ashley in what had been recently rechristened as Kerrytown but had been known as North-Central during the many decades when it was the heart of Black Ann Arbor, one of just a handful of areas of the city where Black families were able to rent or buy a home. Like many young transplants to Ann Arbor, we enjoyed walking up to the Farmers Market and to Zingerman's on Saturday mornings. As someone who aspired to a career in African-American history, I sensed that we were living in what once had been a Black neighborhood, even as it was also clear that the area was changing rapidly. On nice days, elders continued to sit on the front porches of well-kept, small homes. DeLong's Barbecue was still thriving. But for newcomers like us, there was little sign that Ann Street had once been the center of the city's Black Business district. Or that Community High had been, until 1965, Jones School, the city's majority-Black elementary school. On the one hand, there was no sign that the non-descript building at the corner of Fourth and Kingsley had once been the Dunbar Community Center, the vital center of social and recreational life for Ann Arbor's Black children. On the other, Dunbar's successor organization, the Ann Arbor Community Center, continued to operate social service and youth programs in its modern building on North Main Street under the direction of Walter Hill. While the former Second Baptist and Bethel AME church buildings were, and still are, present—Bethel AME has been converted into condominiums and Second Baptist to a childcare center. The congregations had moved decades earlier to new church buildings on John A. Woods Drive and Red Oak Road, respectively.[4]

Of course, much has changed in downtown Ann Arbor in the thirty years since I moved to our city. There is much to the truism that change is the constant in urban environments, even in college towns like ours. To paraphrase a colleague in the BWC, Ann Arbor transplants tend to want to preserve the city as it was when they arrived but struggle to imagine how the city changed in the decades before they arrived. Still, the erasure over the past 50 years of Black Ann Arbor's residential neighborhoods—its businesses, social and cultural institutions, as all as the thriving Black Business district that stood on Ypsilanti's south side—has done real damage to our two cities and all of their residents. It's not just the past that we have lost but also our ability to understand how we reached a present where the city's very real racial and economic inequalities are hidden under a thin veneer of liberal political attitudes.

I want to say a word about why I place such emphasis on segregation when discussing Washtenaw County's racial past and present. When we think of racial segregation, we are taught to think of the laws put in place in the South, beginning in the 1890s, that mandated segregated public schools, public transportation and accommodations, hospitals, cemeteries, and even water fountains. Ann Arbor, of course, never had such laws. In fact, the state of Michigan first banned racial segregation in public education in 1867 and in public accommodations in 1885.[5] Despite these laws, most Black Michiganders could not live wherever they pleased or be served in the restaurant or hotel of their choice. In fact, many communities across Southeast Michigan and across the state effectively barred Black people from residing in their communities. These were sundown towns, communities where Black people were not welcome after the sun went down.[6] And in those cities like Ann Arbor and Ypsilanti where Black families could reside, they were effectively restricted to certain neighborhoods and certain elementary schools. The segregation practiced in Washtenaw County may not have been written into law, but that did not prevent it from constraining Black lives and aspirations.

Residential segregation as policy and practice, but not as law, began in Washtenaw County in the late 19th century. As historian Matthew Siegfried has demonstrated, a concerted effort was made in Ypsilanti to limit Black residences to the South Adams district, the area south of Michigan Avenue and east of Hamilton Street. In 1873, more than one-quarter of Black residences in the city were located north of Michigan Avenue. By 1910, there were only four Black households north of Michigan Avenue, and with the exception of live-in domestic servants, just about every other Black residence in the city was contained within the South Adams district.[7] A similar process of restriction and segregation took place in Ann Arbor. While small numbers of Black families lived in homes across the rural districts surrounding what we now think of as downtown Ann Arbor in the 19th century, by the turn of the 20th century, Black families found themselves unable to rent or purchase homes outside of the boundaries of the North Central and Lower Town neighborhoods. Nor was racial segregation in Washtenaw County limited to housing. Rather, the Ann Arbor and Ypsilanti school districts, industrial plants, and hotels and restaurants all practiced varying levels of racial segregation and discrimination well into the 1940s, 1950s, and 1960s.

How the leaders of Ypsilanti and Ann Arbor enacted and implemented residential segregation is a focus of the BWC's ongoing research. An affiliated project, JusticeInDeed, is in the process of mapping every racial covenant applied to a land deed in the county during the first half of the 20th century.[8] Racial covenants were a tool developed by the real estate industry in the early 20th century to assure white homebuyers that their neighborhoods would remain all-white. In this way, home builders, mortgage loan officers, and real estate agents affirmed that there was real estate value in the whiteness of neighborhoods. Covenants took off as a marketing tool in the 1920s after two Supreme Court rulings. First, in 1917, the court ruled that residential segregation ordinances that had been passed in cities like Louisville, St. Louis, and Baltimore violated the 14th Amendment and were thus unenforceable. Then, in 1923, the court ruled that racial covenants were private contracts not covered by the 14th Amendment and thus could be upheld in the courts.

Research conducted by Mapping Prejudice, a public history project at the University of Minneapolis, has shown how covenants contributed to the process of racial segregation in Minneapolis. As builders and real estate agents promoted racial covenants as a key feature of the many new subdivisions that were going up across the city, white homeowners banded together to drive out the few Black families who had managed to purchase homes in white upper- and middle-income neighborhoods.[9]

Research conducted on racial covenants in Ann Arbor and Ypsilanti to this point suggests that the situation in our communities was somewhat different. Some, but importantly not all, of the subdivisions developed in the two cities in the first half of the 20th century contained racial covenants. For example, all of the new homes built near Ann Arbor's Allmendinger Park and Ypsilanti's Ainsworth Park during the 1920s, 1930s, and 1940s appear to have carried racial covenants. At the same time, homes in well-established, upper-income areas of the two cities—Burns Park and College Heights—show no racial covenants.[10] Why? Our best guess is that the developers of the Allemendinger Park and Ainsworth Park subdivisions were concerned that the proximity of Black neighborhoods would limit the appeal of their new homes to white homebuyers, while the two cities' tight-knit real estate industry and white community leaders did not seem to have viewed racial covenants as necessary to preserve the whiteness of their cities' most elite neighborhoods.

In a similar way, neither city required one of the residential security "red-line" maps commissioned by the federal Home Owners Loan Corporation (HOLC) at the height of the Great Depression. These now-infamous maps evaluated the mortgage lending risk of urban and suburban neighborhoods; red lines were used to designate neighborhoods' racial minority households as high risk. While it may have been that Ann Arbor and Ypsilanti were too small to warrant redlining maps, it also appears that neither city needed a map to ensure federal officials of the racial stability and credit-worthiness of its neighborhoods.[11]

The reason that I have laid out this landscape of racial segregation and discrimination in the county is to ask readers of the extraordinary family histories in this volume to remember the context in which the members of these four families lived their lives and helped to build the institutions that shaped African-American community life in Washtenaw County. The Asher Aray, Bass, Jewett, and Kersey families thrived in spite of the county's racially discriminatory landscape. They thrived because of their resilience and their commitment to hard work, to family and community, and to serving others. We are deeply indebted to the authors of these family histories, the curators of the *Family Foundations* exhibit, and most importantly, to the family members who agreed to share their stories. These histories do more than remind of us how our county and our nation fell short in the past. They help us to understand why we remain, to this day, so far from achieving the ideals of equal opportunity and racial justice. There is much to learn from these histories, but as we learn these histories, we must continually ask ourselves "What is my responsibility to this history and to this community to work for a more just tomorrow?"

Matthew J. Countryman
Associate Professor of Afroamerican & African Studies and History
University of Michigan

THE ASHER ARAY FAMILY

Asher Aray Family Narrative

THE PATRIARCH OF THE ARAY FAMILY comes from New York circa 1670 and relocated to Somerset, New Jersey, before 1708. He then relocated further west to Hunterdon County, New Jersey, about 1729. Aree (Aray) Van Guinea was born more than 100 years before the Revolutionary War—either in Africa (according to the church) or in New Netherland (Manhattan, New York)—to a Dutch master and a slave woman (according to historians). He was a man of mixed-race. He was well-educated and self-sufficient. There is strong evidence that he was born in America. Slaves would not have been taught to read and write. He was an educated man of impeccable social talents and the social skills to earn him respect with his white brothers in colonial America.[12]

Aray Van Guinea's great-grandson Jacob brought his family from New York to the Michigan Territory in 1827. Jacob and his son, James Aray, bought 320 acres of land between 1827 and 1832 within the newly formed county of Washtenaw, Michigan. The Aray family owned many acres of land in Pittsfield Township by 1832. Michigan would not become a state until January 26, 1837.

Jacob's son, Asher, married Catherine Watts in 1831. He purchased 80 acres of land on both sides of the Chicago Road (now US-12), immediately west of the present US-23. In that day, US 12 was an unimproved, often muddy, Native American trail soon to become the major east-west route in Michigan. It was on this property he and Catherine started to enjoy their roles as Underground Railroad (UGRR) conductors—transporters of escaped slaves seeking their freedom in nearby Canada. They were aided in their efforts by neighbors and other citizens who held the same belief that all men deserved to be free.

Asher was a staunch abolitionist. He and his brother James signed with a group of abolitionists pledging support for the movement. Their names, and many other well-known local names, were published in the *Signal of Liberty* newspaper in May 1843. The Underground Railroad movement was a very secretive, tight-knit group of people risking their land, their family's safety, and even their lives to help escaping slaves to the Detroit River for a boat ride to freedom just a short distance away.

One of the documented slave escapes also happened to be the largest effort to assist freedom seekers in their quest for freedom. "The Escape of the 28" from Kentucky into Ohio, Indiana, and Michigan was a daring gamble to move a large group of freedom seekers to Detroit and ultimately to Canada. Their operation was known as the "Fairfield 28."[13] Their final stop before Detroit was the farms of Asher Aray, William Harwood, and Roswell Preston. The journey was a success, and messengers were sent ahead to Detroit to herald their arrival. Protection was planned, supplies were gathered, and they set sail, singing, headed for the Canadian shore where the dream of freedom became a reality.[14]

As mentioned, some of Asher's neighbors assisted Asher in his efforts. Most notably was William Webb Harwood. His farm is now a Michigan Centennial Farm. The house was refurbished by the State of Michigan, and it was determined that there is evidence of UGRR usage. Roswell Preston was another neighbor of Asher. His property adjoined with Asher's in the 1850s.

Quoting from the biography of Captain Roswell Preston:

Roswell's nearest neighbor was Asher Aray, an intelligent and a prosperous Negro, who, with his family, owned and operated the adjoining farm. That Negro's farm was one of the stations on the Underground Railroad. Fugitive Slaves traveled by night. During the daytime, they were hiding and resting. They sometimes came singly; more frequently in gangs of three or more and, on one occasion, farmer Aray had twenty fugitives who were fed and secreted about his premises in a single day.[15]

It is my personal belief that another neighbor assisted in the UGRR effort. He was also a neighbor of Asher's, Benjamin Day. Benjamin came to the Michigan Territory possibly with the Arays.[16] There is no documentation that Benjamin was involved in the UGRR. The whole operation was so secretive. The Fairfield 28 escape took place in April 1853. In August of 1854, Asher allowed Martha Aray, his oldest daughter, to be married to Benjamin Day, a neighbor and possibly a hired hand on the Aray farm operation.

Asher's neighbors assisted him in a variety of ways. They would loan him horses or wagons to help with his efforts. They provided their farms so fugitive slaves could rest and be fed. The Slave Act of 1850 dictated that anyone found assisting runaway slaves could be taken to court. This placed even assistants in danger of losing their farms, equipment, personal freedom, and livelihood.

Asher and others stood defiant as a team. He was a resourceful and dignified man defying "the law" so that once-enslaved people could realize their thirst, dreams, and longing for freedom. North Buxton, Ontario, was their destination, which provided a safe haven and a support system for freed slaves.

They still have a North Buxton Homecoming at the historic site of North Buxton, Ontario, every Labor Day weekend, where people can research their roots and touch base with long-lost relatives and establish new friendships.

One final note, Asher and Catherine had seven children, five of whom grew to adulthood. I still have contact with three descendents of Asher Aray's children. Linda Williams-Bowie is descended from Eglon Aray, born in 1844. Patricia (Brown) Whitsett and Karmen Brown are descended from James W. Aray, born in 1832. I am descended from Martha (Aray) Day, born in 1835.

The Asher Aray Family

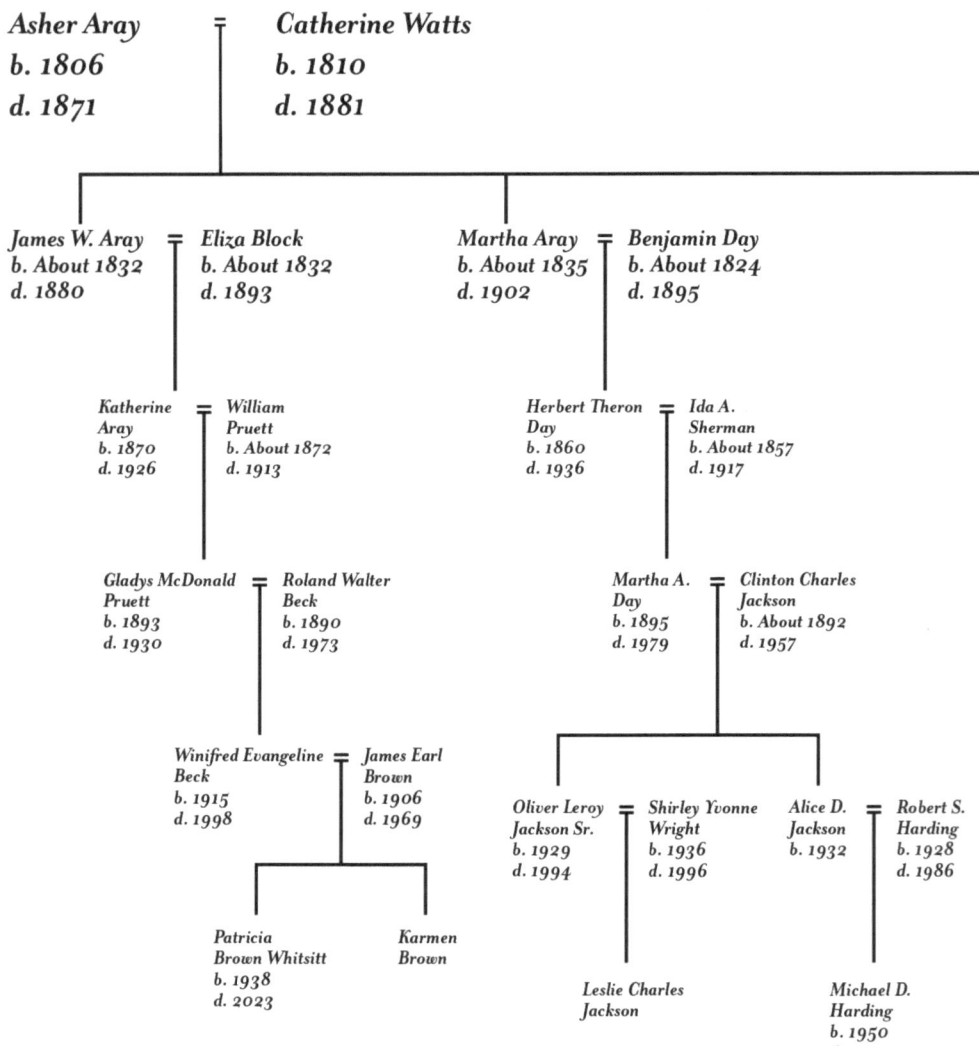

Asher Aray
b. 1806
d. 1871

Catherine Watts
b. 1810
d. 1881

James W. Aray
b. About 1832
d. 1880

Eliza Block
b. About 1832
d. 1893

Martha Aray
b. About 1835
d. 1902

Benjamin Day
b. About 1824
d. 1895

Katherine
Aray
b. 1870
d. 1926

William
Pruett
b. About 1872
d. 1913

Herbert Theron
Day
b. 1860
d. 1936

Ida A.
Sherman
b. About 1857
d. 1917

Gladys McDonald
Pruett
b. 1893
d. 1930

Roland Walter
Beck
b. 1890
d. 1973

Martha A.
Day
b. 1895
d. 1979

Clinton Charles
Jackson
b. About 1892
d. 1957

Winifred Evangeline
Beck
b. 1915
d. 1998

James Earl
Brown
b. 1906
d. 1969

Oliver Leroy
Jackson Sr.
b. 1929
d. 1994

Shirley Yvonne
Wright
b. 1936
d. 1996

Alice D.
Jackson
b. 1932

Robert S.
Harding
b. 1928
d. 1986

Patricia
Brown Whitsitt
b. 1938
d. 2023

Karmen
Brown

Leslie Charles
Jackson

Michael D.
Harding
b. 1950
d. 2012

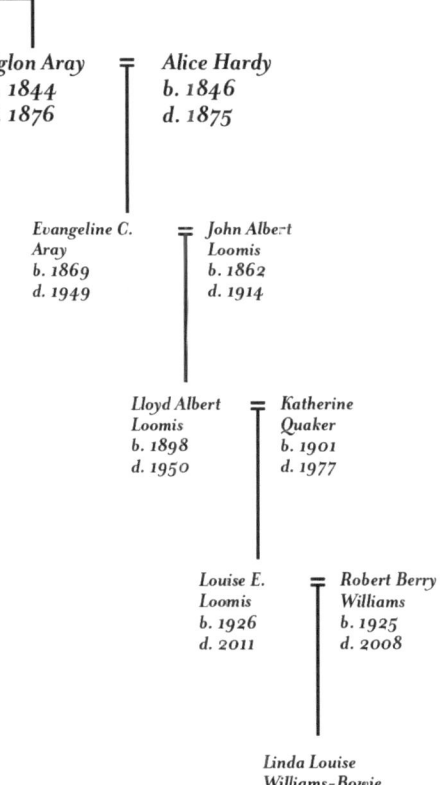

Eglon Aray = *Alice Hardy*
b. 1844   *b. 1846*
d. 1876   *d. 1875*

Evangeline C. = *John Albert*
Aray   *Loomis*
b. 1869   *b. 1862*
d. 1949   *d. 1914*

Lloyd Albert = *Katherine*
Loomis   *Quaker*
b. 1898   *b. 1901*
d. 1950   *d. 1977*

Louise E. = *Robert Berry*
Loomis   *Williams*
b. 1926   *b. 1925*
d. 2011   *d. 2008*

Linda Louise
Williams-Bowie

Interview with Alice Gilbert and Les Jackson

LES JACKSON: I'm Les Jackson. I'm a descendant of Asher Aray.

ALICE GILBERT: I'm Alice Gilbert, a descendant of Asher Aray.

JOYCE HUNTER: Great. We have four questions. I'm going to start with the first one. Can you describe your family tree and ancestry?

LES JACKSON: Yeah. Our family tree is quite extensive. Asher Aray is our third great-grandfather, and he was the son of Jacob Aray and Berthena West. They came to the Michigan Territory in 1827, and Jacob Aray and Berthena—they had four children, and they settled in Pittsfield Township, near the intersection of what is now known as 23 and US-12. Back then, US-12 was basically an Indian trail. All the roads, or a lot of the roads in the state, were built from the old Indian trails. And traveling on US-12 was no piece of cake. It was muddy, it was trenched. It had to be widened. They had lumbermen come in and widen the path. And they widened the path so that they could get more than just two people walking side by side because these were Indian trails. This was the basic development in the Michigan Territory at that time. And right around 1824, I believe, they appropriated funds to try to widen Michigan Avenue or US-12, the Old Chicago Road, so that they could pass more traffic on the road. Back then, it was just exceedingly difficult. Like I said, the roads weren't really roads, they were just trails. The towns and the population sprung up around these trails, so much to the story.

JOYCE HUNTER: Well, that's a good start. You can always add to it, but I wanted to see if your Aunt Alice wanted to add anything about the family tree and ancestry.

ALICE GILBERT: Yes. I'm Alice Jackson Gilbert and 90 years old plus. I am a descendant of Asher Aray. That's about all I can say right now; that'll come to my remembering.

JOYCE HUNTER: You have a very strong voice. It's great.

ALICE GILBERT: I've always been a person that lived on East Cross Street, and I'm still living on East Cross Street.

JOYCE HUNTER: And how long have you lived there?

ALICE GILBERT: I'm 90 years old. [LAUGHTER] A portion of that time, when I was younger and married, I lived in Romulus, Michigan. But I returned back to Ypsilanti.

LES JACKSON: There's a piece of property on East Cross Street that has been in the family for 107 years, 108 years?

JOYCE HUNTER: Okay.

LES JACKSON: Herbert Day. I'm going to talk a little bit about the tree.

JOYCE HUNTER: Go ahead.

LES JACKSON: Alice Jackson Gilbert was the daughter of Martha Day Jackson and Clinton Jackson. Martha Day Jackson was the daughter of Herbert Theron Day and Ida Adelle Sherman. Herbert Day was the son of Benjamin Day and Martha Aray Day, and Martha Aray was Asher's daughter. There's strong speculation that Benjamin Day assisted Asher Aray in the Underground Railroad. He was a very large man, and there's no doubt in my mind that he assisted in Asher's efforts in transporting and hiding slaves, but there's no documentation. Carol Mull has been looking for documentation on this for years. Carol Mull wrote the book *The Underground Railroad in Michigan*. Right around 1968, there was a fire at Alice's mother's house, and it completely destroyed the house. I remember photographs hanging on the stairwell and in the other rooms and just beautiful photographs, large photographs. I remember I was a little pensive going up the stairs because Asher Aray was staring down at you [LAUGHTER] from this big photograph that was under a bubble of glass. It was pretty impressive. But anyway, that house burned, and there's a lot of documentation that burned with it. We really don't have any artifacts from the era.

JOYCE HUNTER: So I'm going to go on to the next question, and whenever you want to go back, you can also go back and add to it.

LES JACKSON: Okay.

JOYCE HUNTER: How did your family arrive in the Ann Arbor / Ypsilanti / Washtenaw County area?

LES JACKSON: Most likely they came by boat. The Erie Canal was finished. Well, about 1824, the Erie Canal was finished, and it made travel to Michigan a lot easier. Traveling by land was okay, but getting up into Michigan from Ohio, there was a huge bog that prevented people from traveling north out of Ohio and made it very difficult for travel over land. Here again, Carol Mull speculates that the Days and the Geddes, maybe the Harwoods and a whole group of people, came over via the Erie Canal, docked in Detroit, and made their way westward to Pittsfield Township. The Aray family had owned property in Pittsfield Township before they got there. There's documentation that James Aray bought 80 acres of land in Pittsfield Township, January or February of 1827. The Arays, I think, they arrived in probably June or July of 1827. They had land to stay on. There's just this huge question as to who this "James Aray" was because James Aray was also one of Asher's sons. James Aray was also one of Asher's brothers, and James Aray was Asher's uncle. Asher's uncle fought in the Revolutionary War for the New Jersey regiment in the Continental Army. There's speculation that he had a land grant for this property. I got a statement from 1818 that James Aray made to the War Department looking for assistance. It was very possible that he could have gotten a land grant, which is where this land came from, but we don't have any real documentation on that. That's one of the big sticking points that I'm trying to research so that I can figure this out. But James Aray was a very common name in the Aray family.

JOYCE HUNTER: Okay. I'm going to move to the next question. You already talked about that, but we'll go over it again. Were there any local places of importance for your family? It mentions here: describe the place and its importance. I know you mentioned Cross Street, do you want to talk about that a little bit more?

LES JACKSON: Yeah. The address at the time was 614 East Cross Street, and Herbert Day apparently sold some property from the Aray family because he was in the lineage of inheritance. He bought four pieces of property. He bought 614 East Cross Street, which was a farmhouse, and it was part of the Gilbert estate back then. Herbert Day also bought the house next door, which was 620 East Cross Street. Then the third piece of property he bought was on Miles Street, M-I-L-E-S, and that address was, I believe, it was 224. My grandmother Martha, her sister lived there. Lillian Bradley lived in that house. Later in life, Herbert Day and Ida Sherman lived with Lillian and Benjamin Bradley over on Miles Street. The fourth piece of property was out in Waldron, Michigan, in Hillsdale County, I believe. During the Depression, Herbert Day moved his family down to Waldron, Michigan, to live on their farm so that they could support themselves. Do you have any remembrances of Waldron out there?

ALICE GILBERT: Oh, no. I remember a country road that I was often on, but that's about it.

JOYCE HUNTER: So Miles Street, that property could be a picture or something we could use as part of the exhibit, is that right?

LES JACKSON: Yeah. I think you can find a photo of the house.

JOYCE HUNTER: That would be great. I'm going to go to the final question and that is: are there any people, artifacts, or pictures unique to your family that you would like to share? I know we've asked you to collect items for the exhibit. Is there anything special you'd like to share or talk about?

LES JACKSON: Yes.

JOYCE HUNTER: Go ahead.

LES JACKSON: Aunt Alice's brother, Clinton Herbert Jackson, he was an officer in the army and he fought in World War II, and he also fought in Korea. There's a book I have at home called, I can't think of the name. I think it's *The River and the Gauntlet*. In that book, it describes the battle where the United States—or I'll say the United Nations forces—the United Nations forces were forced to retreat from probably 50 miles from the Chinese border all the way back to the 38th Parallel. I'm still working on documentation, but General MacArthur told President Truman that the troops would be home by Christmas. This was dubbed as the Home by Christmas campaign. They moved easily up into North Korea on the night of November 24, 1950; the Chinese attacked, and they just slaughtered the American forces. American forces weren't prepared. In the book, it talks about supply issues, it talks about ammunition deficiencies and a lot of shortcomings the intelligence just dropped the ball on. It was really an embarrassment. But Clinton Herbert Day, he was captured in that battle in 1950, and in January 31, 1951, the Army declared him as deceased as a POW. He earned the Silver Star and some other medals. He was an officer of a mixed-race unit in Korea, which was just getting off the ground during that period of time. But we have a picture of him. I'm putting together a picture frame with all those medals, and we'd like to donate that to the museum.

JOYCE HUNTER: Thank you for that. But I want to—before we sound off, I want to see if your Aunt Alice has anything she wants to say or add.

ALICE GILBERT: No, I really can't. Being 90-plus, I'm just about thinking of today.

JOYCE HUNTER: Okay, I understand. Anything about your childhood that you'd like to share?

ALICE GILBERT: Well, I can remember that we were, as I can recall, we were the only Black family there in that area.

LES JACKSON: When Herbert Day bought that property on East Cross Street, he met up with a lot of resistance.

JOYCE HUNTER: I understand that. Certainly.

Asher Aray

Catherine   *Martha*   *Eglon Aray*   *Herbert*   *Ida Adele*
Watts   *(Aray) Day*   *Theron Day*   *Sherman*

Eglon and Alice (Hardy) Aray

Martha Amelia Day

Clinton Charles Jackson

The Benjamin Day family. Left to right: Martha (Aray) Day, Alice June Day, Benjamin Day, Herbert Theron Day

Katherine L. Aray

Evangeline (Aray) Loomis

H. Aray Loomis
(Ypsilanti Historical Society)

Lloyd A. Loomis

Gladys McDonald Pruett

Unidentified Aray descendant

Unidentified Aray descendant

Unidentified Aray descendant

Unidentified Aray descendant

Unidentified Aray descendant

Cecil Eugene Jackson

Charlotte Clarissa Marie Jackson

Oliver Leroy Jackson Sr.

Sharon Shirley Jackson

Frederick Edsel Jackson

1. Adrienne Flowers; 2. Araina Flowers; 3. Chole Whitsett; 4. Chawn Whitsett;
5. Chauné Rael-Whitsett; 6. Karmen Brown; 7. Patricia (Brown) Whitsett;
8. Angela Burton; 9. Cheah Rael-Whitsett; 10. Adonis Wilson-Whitsett;
11. Cienna Rael-Whitsett

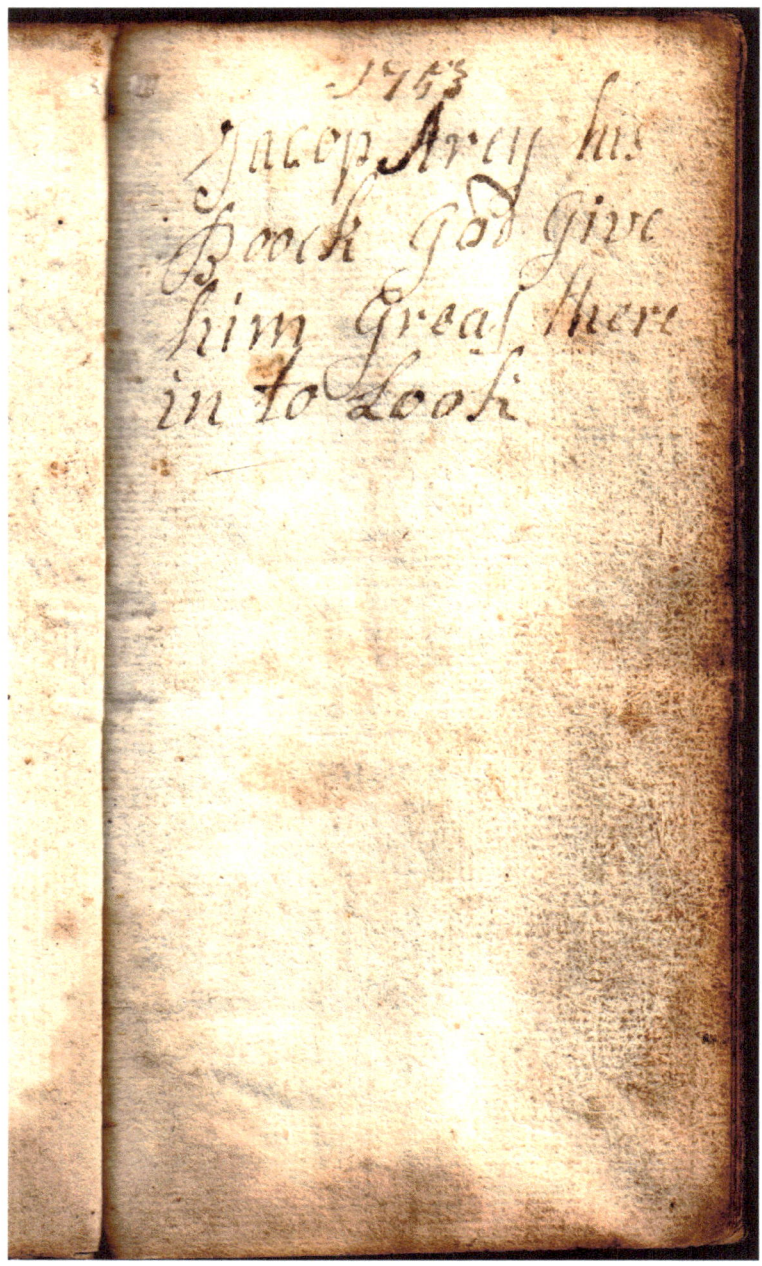

Pages from Old Dutch Aray Family Bible, in the possession of Mrs. Ladell Wyatt. The oldest written date is 1753.

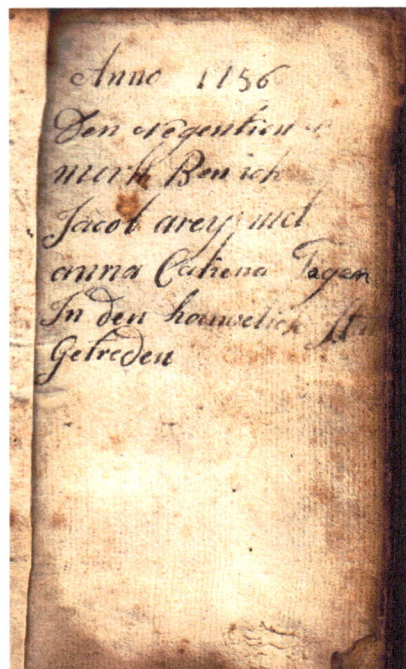
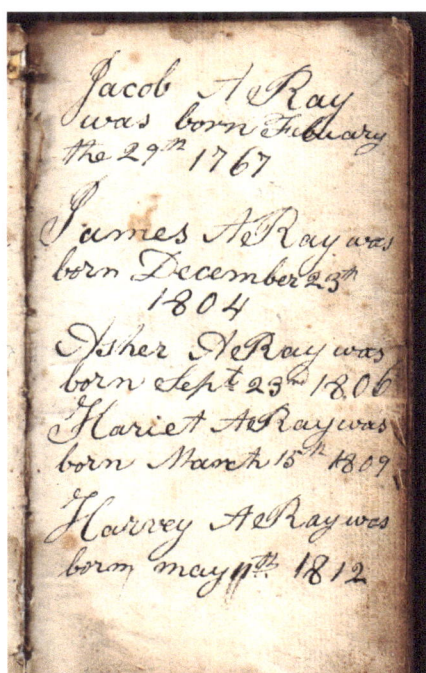

Pages from Old Dutch Aray Family Bible, in the possession of Mrs. Ladell Wyatt. The oldest written date is 1753.

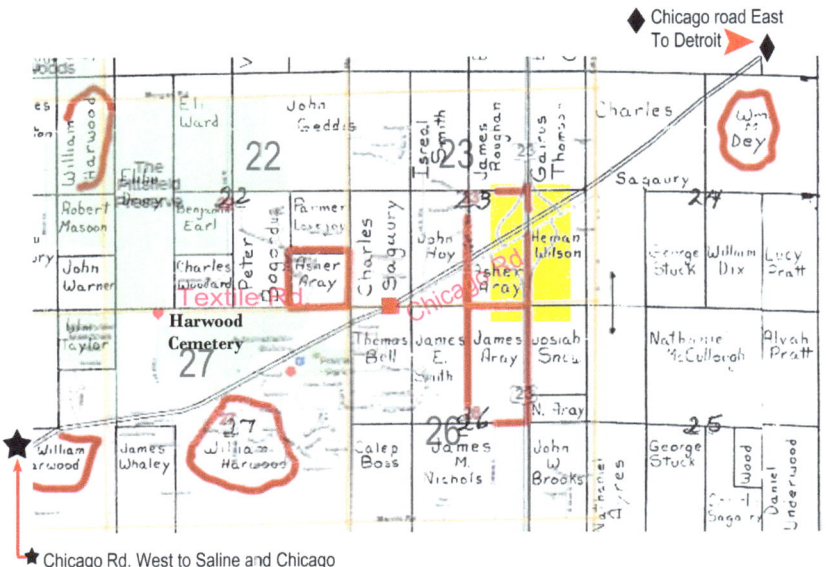

Composite map of 1840 plat (red sections) and 2000 plat (green and yellow sections) of Pittsfield Township

Certificate.
No. 2400

The United States of America,

To all to whom these presents shall come, Greeting :

Whereas, James Aray, of Genesee county, New York,

has deposited in the General Land Office of the United States, a certificate of the Register of the Land Office at Detroit,

whereby it appears that full payment has been made by the said James Aray

according to the provisions of the Act of Congress of the 24th of April, 1820, entitled "An act making further provision for the sale of the Public Lands," for

the East half of the North west quarter of Section thirteen, in township three South, of Range

six East, in the district of Lands offered for sale at Detroit, Michigan Territory, containing

eighty acres

according to the official plat of the survey of the said Lands, returned to the General Land Office by the Surveyor General, which said tract has been pur-

chased by the said James Aray

NOW KNOW YE, That the **UNITED STATES OF AMERICA,** in consideration of the premises, and in conformity with the several

acts of Congress, in such case made and provided, have Given and Granted, and, by these presents, do give and grant, unto the said James Aray

and to his heirs   the said tract above described : To Have and to Hold the same, together with all the rights, privileges, immunities and appur-

tenances, of whatsoever nature thereto belonging, unto the said James Aray

and to his   heirs and assigns forever.

In testimony whereof, I, John Quincy Adams

PRESIDENT OF THE UNITED STATES OF AMERICA, have caused these letters to be made Patent, and the seal of the General Land Office to be hereunto

affixed.

Given under my hand, at the City of Washington, the first   day of May   in the year of our

Lord, one thousand eight hundred and twenty eight   and of the Independence of the United States the

fifty first

By the President, — J. Q. A.

S. S.

Commissioner of the General Land Office.

THE BASS FAMILY

Bass Family Narrative

THOMAS BASS DELIVERED practically all the Black babies born in Ypsilanti after opening his practice in 1943. During the same years, his wife, Louise Bass, was a well-respected mathematics teacher at East Junior High School (eventually to become East Middle School). Dr. and Mrs. Bass were committed to changing the world one person at a time. Their commitment to public service and the Ypsilanti community was shaped by the racism and struggles they had both faced during their youth. On many occasions, they recounted the support and encouragement they received from members of their church, family friends, teachers, and college professors. For both, their mission was to pay it forward to those struggling. They kept their doors open and their shoulders broad and tall for those who needed assistance to climb up.

Dr. Bass had practiced medicine in several other communities before coming to the University of Michigan to get a degree in public health. He opened a temporary office in Ypsilanti's public housing, which was open in the evening. The prior doctor serving Ypsilanti's Black community was in deteriorating health, so Dr. Bass decided to stay. "Doc," as he was lovingly called by all, was a proud member of Alpha Phi Alpha, the oldest intercollegiate historically Black fraternity, and a graduate of the famous Eastside High School featured in the film *Lean on Me*. He was a proud alumnus of Lincoln University and Meharry Medical College and interned at Howard University's Freedmen's Hospital. He attended the University of Michigan's School of Public Health and quickly realized this was not going to provide opportunities that would enable him to fight the racism that he clearly saw in the medical community and impact the quality of medical care available to the Black community.

Louise Bass was a graduate of Hampton University and went on to receive an MA from Eastern Michigan University. She truly excelled at math and became the consummate teacher. She was held in high esteem by her colleagues and all the people she touched. She loved recounting her college adventures and the many jobs she worked to pay her way through school. She babysat, cleaned, and washed, and ironed clothes to earn money to pay college fees. Her village in Dayton, Ohio, never stopped supporting her with letters and funds to close the gap between her meager earnings and the financial obligations she faced. "Ma Bass" initially made herself available to the community by creating a nursery school and then moving on to teach at Ypsilanti's East Junior High School and then as a tutor until she passed away in 1992. People of all races and ages stopped by to sit at the card table in the Bass home, ask for advice, and benefit from her knowledge, guidance, and inspiration. Upon her passing, there was an article in the Ypsilanti Press titled "Ypsi woman mourned as one who touched many people"—a fitting description of her contribution to the community.

Both Thomas and Louise Bass were interested in public service and became involved in almost every group that served the Black community, including the Boy Scouts, Girl Scouts, the local NAACP chapter, Ypsilanti Association of Women's Clubs, Washtenaw County United Fund, Michigan Literacy, Inc., Ypsi Voguettes, Palm Leaf Club, the Urban League, and their church, Brown Chapel AME. In addition to their work in clubs and organizations, they built a formidable library in their home featuring books by Black authors, including James Baldwin, Toni Morrison, Langston Hughes, Alice Walker, Claude Brown, John Hope Franklin, and others. Dr. Bass attended the March on Washington for Jobs and Freedom in 1963 with his daughter Ann and forever carried the words of Dr. Martin Luther King Jr. in his heart.

Their son, Michael Bass, excelled in almost every sport at Ypsilanti High School. He was an honor roll student and graduated in 1963 as the first Black senior class president in the school's history. He went on to play football for the University of Michigan, graduating in 1967.

Michael was drafted into the NFL to play for the Green Bay Packers, then the Detroit Lions, until Coach Vince Lombardi recruited him to the Washington Redskins, where he spent the rest of his 10-year NFL career. Michael has been named as one of the 70 greatest Redskins players and in 2022 was inducted into the Washington Commanders Ring of Fame, with his name engraved in the stadium. Mr. Bass was also a history teacher at Willow Run High School for a brief time.

Their daughter, Ann Bass, was one of the first Black homecoming queens at Ypsilanti High School. She has enjoyed a successful career as a special education teacher and administrator with a BA from Eastern Michigan University and an advanced degree from the University of Michigan. She retired from Wayne-Westland Community Schools and continues serving her community by tutoring.

Their youngest daughter, Dr. Leah Bass-Baylis, has enjoyed a career as a dancer, singer, actress, and choreographer and performed on the 1996 Academy Awards. She was the dance captain of the Broadway hit *The Tap Dance Kid* and has toured nationally and internationally with luminaries such as Richard Roundtree, Debbie Allen, Eartha Kitt, and Morgan Freeman. She was the first Dance Specialist for the Los Angeles Unified School District and possesses a BA from Spelman College, an MA from Teachers College, Columbia University, an MS from Pepperdine University, and a doctoral degree from the University of Southern California.. She is currently providing arts education consulting services in the metropolitan Los Angeles area.

The Bass Family

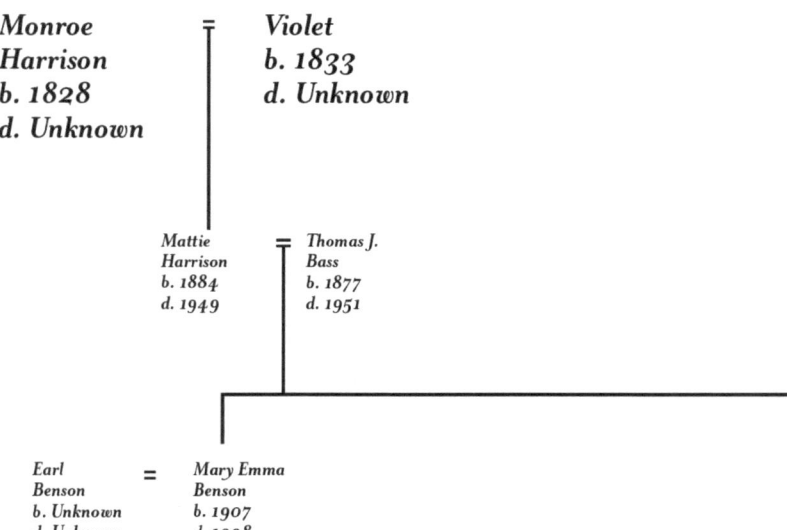

Monroe
Harrison
b. 1828
d. Unknown

Violet
b. 1833
d. Unknown

Mattie
Harrison
b. 1884
d. 1949

Thomas J.
Bass
b. 1877
d. 1951

Earl
Benson
b. Unknown
d. Unknown

Mary Emma
Benson
b. 1907
d. 1998

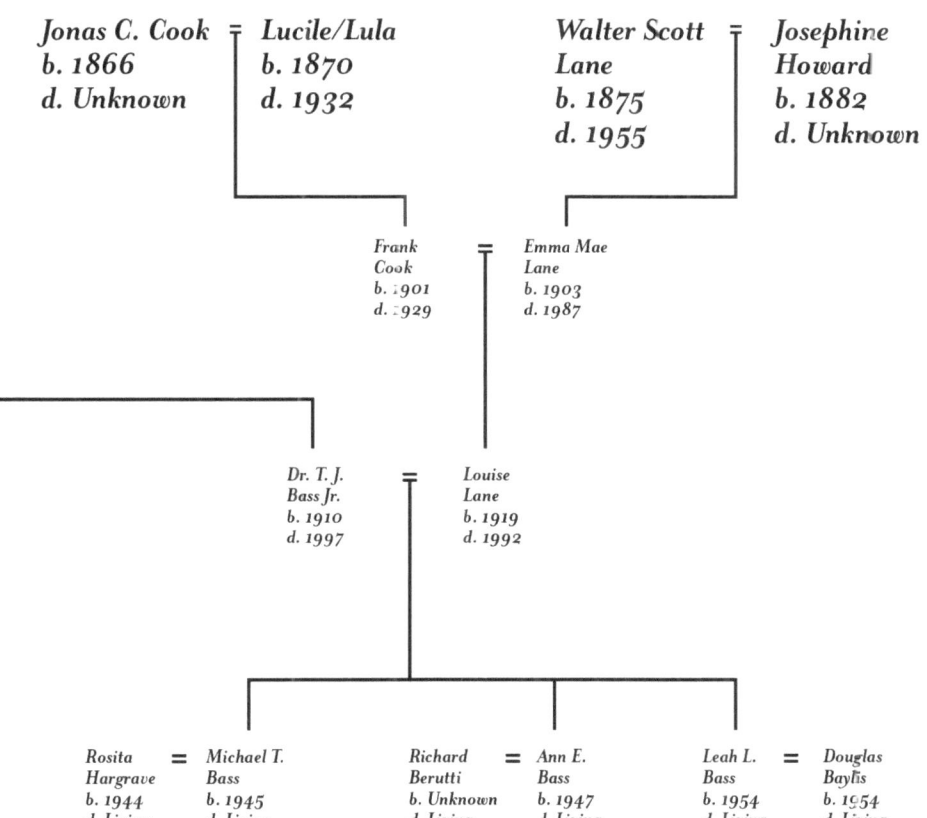

Jonas C. Cook
b. 1866
d. Unknown
=
Lucile/Lula
b. 1870
d. 1932

Walter Scott
Lane
b. 1875
d. 1955
=
Josephine
Howard
b. 1882
d. Unknown

Frank
Cook
b. 1901
d. 1929
=
Emma Mae
Lane
b. 1903
d. 1987

Dr. T. J.
Bass Jr.
b. 1910
d. 1997
=
Louise
Lane
b. 1919
d. 1992

Rosita
Hargrave
b. 1944
d. Living
=
Michael T.
Bass
b. 1945
d. Living

Richard
Berutti
b. Unknown
d. Living
=
Ann E.
Bass
b. 1947
d. Living

Leah L.
Bass
b. 1954
d. Living
=
Douglas
Baylis
b. 1954
d. Living

Interview with Mike Bass

MIKE BASS: My name is Mike Bass, and I'm a descendant of Louise and Dr. Thomas J. Bass of Ypsilanti. My dad was originally from Paterson, New Jersey, and my mom was born in Auburn, Arkansas.

JOYCE HUNTER: Mike, thank you for doing the interview, and thank you for being part of this upcoming exhibit. We're so excited about it. We're going to start with the first question, which is: can you describe your family tree and ancestry?

MIKE BASS: Well, it's somewhat limited. On my dad's side, we know that my grandfather, his father, was born around 1872-73 in Antigua. Quite frankly, he boarded the ship as a stowaway and traveled to New York, and there, he jumped ship. My dad was born in 1910, and it's been history ever since. My mom, who was born in Arkansas, and she was born in 1919, spent much of her time in St. Louis before her and my grandma, Emma Kent, moved to Dayton, Ohio. My sisters and I are in the process of trying to do our family tree, but that's quite an endeavor. Fortunately though, we have some people on both sides who are looking at all of these things, who are more adept than I am in going through all of this. But we're so very thankful, my sisters and I, for the parents that we had. Very fortunate. They understood all of the trials and tribulations that most Black people went through in the early 1900s, all the way up to when I was born and my sisters were born, which was in '40s, and then my youngest sister in 1954. But from that time, my sisters and I have continued to feel just how fortunate we were to have the parents that we had.

JOYCE HUNTER: You touched on that just a minute ago, but how did your family arrive in the Ann Arbor / Ypsilanti / Washtenaw County area?

MIKE BASS: Well, my dad went to the university at Lincoln University in Pennsylvania, and then he went to med school at Meharry in Tennessee. After graduating from Meharry, he actually settled in River Rouge. He was there for several years and decided to open up his practice, though, in Ypsilanti. That's where he met my mom, who was actually associated with Eastern Michigan at the time. I think it was called Normal at the time. They got married, and we grew up, actually, on the south side of Ypsilanti, in an area that is called Parkridge, the projects, and so forth, but it's changed quite a bit. But early on, that's where we grew up, and most of my life was spent on Harriet Street, and the rest is history. Dad, at the very beginning, was one of two Black doctors in Ypsilanti. The original doctor was Dr. Clark. When Dr. Clark passed away, my dad, for a number of years, was the only Black doctor in the Ypsilanti area. But during that whole period of growing up, we had a very sound foundation. Quite frankly, we didn't feel like we had lost out on anything, and I think this is a tribute to how my sisters and I were raised by my mom and dad. They were proponents of education, and as a result, so are my sisters and I. The key to education—the key to any success is based on the foundation of education.

JOYCE HUNTER: Mike, tell me a little bit about—I know when we interviewed you before, you talked about your father making house calls and that so many people knew your father. Can you talk about that a little bit?

MIKE BASS: He was the original GP, and he constantly was making house calls. I remember helping him pack his bag when he had to go to these calls, and he was dedicated to his profession. He really wanted to help people. For a long time, he didn't even have an office, he worked out of the place that we lived at in Parkridge. Time and time again, he would make these house calls, and a lot of times he didn't expect to get paid, but he certainly appreciated the sweet potato pie or the chicken dinner, and he took that instead of the actual money. He was very proud of that because he was dedicated to his profession. The many times I went with him as the oldest in the family—and there was some very good times, and there were some sad times as well. As for a period of time, he was the county medical examiner, and often times, he had to pronounce people dead and so forth, which was interesting to me, and at the time, I just had to listen, and I understood the grief that accompanied someone passing away. But he developed a following, and I think is personified by just how well respected he was and still is in the Ypsilanti community.

JOYCE HUNTER: Also, I think I recall, you mentioned your mother being involved with, or instrumental in, opening or moving forward on, the Parkridge Community Center. Can you talk about that a little bit?

MIKE BASS: Yes. Like I said, I had two sisters, an older one—Anne, who was two years younger than me; and then my youngest sister, Leah, who's nine years younger than I am. But early on it was, for a while, just my older sister Anne and I. My mom didn't really work, actually, until we got in high school. During that period of time of our growing up, she was very active in the community and particularly active with the young girls at the time. She started a Girl Scout troop; she started a club called The Teenagers. Many of those girls at the time became my babysitters, particularly the Frierson girls, and also Mary Louise Foley and a number of others. Miss VanSlyke. There are just a number of them. I grew up with the old saying that it takes a village, and as a result, if I wanted to, I couldn't do anything wrong because it didn't take very long for my mom to know just exactly what I might have done that I shouldn't have done. We were constantly on our Ps and Qs. But we felt the love of the community. We also felt the respect that my mother, in particular, had earned among these young women in the community.

MIKE BASS: She remained very, very close friends and a guiding light for many of them. I still recall so many of them who constantly have referred to her, as well as a number of the students who, after we went into high school, my mom decided to go back and teach school. She was a teacher for a number of years at the then East Side Junior High School. Even periodically, when I might post something on Facebook, many of her former students would have very kind things to say about her. It just made me feel good that she was able to make those contributions, not only to the girls in the community but also her students as well.

JOYCE HUNTER: Were there any local places of importance for your family? If so, please describe the place and why it was important to your ancestors.

MIKE BASS: The first thing that I can think of is the AME Church on Adams Street. That was a meeting place for all of us, and my mom and dad were members, and my sisters and I joined as soon as we could understand the benefits of religion and the guidance that religion could give us in leading a productive life. I would say that the AME Church on Adams really played an important part in our upbringing. The other thing that was so important was the Parkridge Community Center. That was on Harriet Street as well, and it was just up the street from where we actually grew up, and it was the meeting place for just about every activity on the south side of town. Jesse Rutherford was the director at the time, and there was just something happening there at Parkridge almost every day, and we looked forward to going there on Friday evenings for our dance and dancing and getting together. The third thing was the Perry School which, at that time when we were growing up, was known as the Harriet Street School but, again, the majority of almost all of the students there were all Black, and Mr. Charles Beatty was the principal at the time, and I can remember all of those teachers who we had were consistently reminding us of how important it was that we pay attention, that we follow instructions, that we remain respectful, and that we do the very best that we can when it comes to education. Finally, the fourth thing that I continued to appreciate was the fact that we had Little League baseball, and it was always exciting for us to go to recreation parks where we had not only school activities every year but where I learned to play baseball, and that was my first actual experience in athletics because it was the central place for all of us. That's the first time that we really came in contact with a lot of white kids. Fortunately, because of the teachers that we had, we were not as ignorant, you might say, of the fact that there were people who were different from us but no better, and that was important as well.

JOYCE HUNTER: Mike, you mentioned the AME Church, so you're referring to Brown Chapel AME, is that correct?

MIKE BASS: Correct, yes. They've since built a new church there on Michigan Avenue. But at the time that we were growing up, it was Brown Chapel there on Adams, and I very much recall Mrs. Kersey, and I've seen pictures of her when she taught at the Harriet Street Elementary School, as well as her being the organist at Brown Chapel. What a fine lady.

JOYCE HUNTER: Are there any people, artifacts, or pictures unique to your family that you would like to share?

MIKE BASS: Well, in terms of photographs, I always remember the photograph of my mom and dad together later on in life. Everything was so positive around our household and fortunately, and sometimes I wonder if it wasn't a curse, my mom and dad actually emphasize the fact that we were going to participate in everything that occurred in Ypsilanti. In so many instances, my sisters and I were the only Black people who participated in these things. Not only in swimming lessons but other things as well, but I remember, constantly, that my mom and dad emphasized that no matter what the situation was, we were equal to anybody and that it was important to us that we not have any prejudice whatsoever, even at this time. I remember, and I'm 78 years old, of her saying to me "Michael," and that's what she and my dad always called me, "Michael, you do not want to be prejudiced. You don't want to have any bigotry. As a matter of fact being prejudiced is a sign of ignorance." At five years old, she was saying, "Michael, you don't want to be ignorant, do you?" That sticks with me all these many years. I've developed an attitude of trying to judge every person by the way that they judge or interact with me. We all have our prejudices, but being able to put yourself on the other side and trying not to give off the bad vibes that some people have a tendency to do, I think it's helped all of us quite a bit.

JOYCE HUNTER: Thank you, Mike. That concludes our interview.

Longtime Teacher Louise Bass Serves As Mentor For Ypsilanti Youth, April 1989

Louise Bass, 1936   *Louise Bass, c. 1943*   *Louise Bass, 1972*

Dr. Thomas Bass, 1936   *Dr. Thomas Bass, 1978*   *Dr. Thomas Bass, 1991*

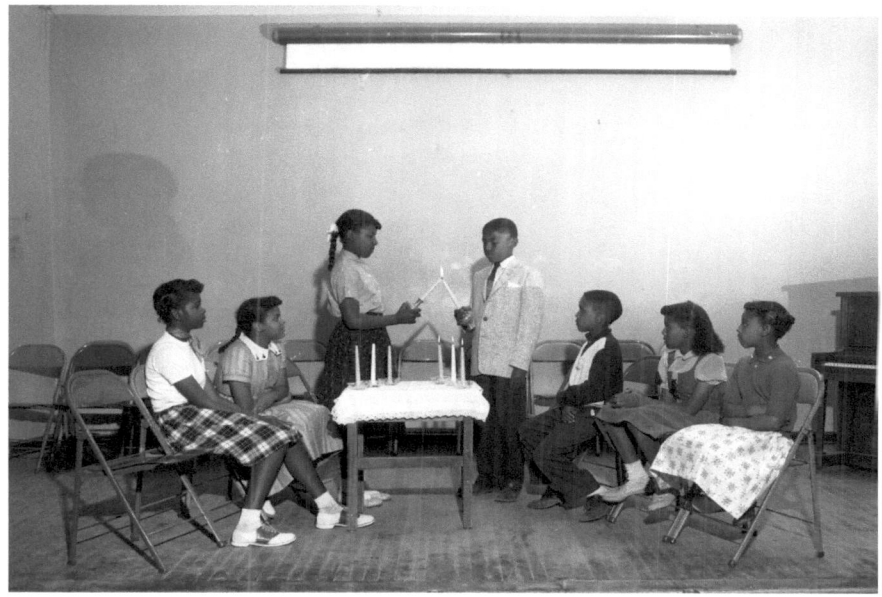

Fifth grader Mike Bass and sixth grader Rosita Hargrave join candles at the
Student Council Officers Installation Ceremony at Harriet School, Ypsilanti,
May 1956. Later in life, Mike and Rosita became a couple and got married.

Mike Bass, UM Football   *Circa 1950-Mike (5years)*
                                            & Ann (3years)

Ypsilanti Hosts Appreciation Banquet For Thomas and Louise Bass, December 1979

Leah Bass Baylis & President Bill Clinton, circa 1990s

Mike & Rosita, 1956

Mike & Rosita, 1966

*Callanwolde Dancer
Leah Bass, circa 1970s*

*Leah Bass Baylis, Principal of Carlos
Santana Arts Academy, circa 2010s*

*Leah Bass Baylis and Pope
John Paul II, Circa 1980s*

*Leah Bass and Debbie Allen,
Circa 2022*

Mike Bass and President Richard Nixon

Left: Rosita, Cornelious & JJ 2018. Right: Rosita, JJ & Cornelious 2023

Bass has stressed youth development

Volunteer of the week

By JO COLLINS MATHIS
Press Lifestyle Editor

For 36 years, Thomas Bass has helped see to it that the young people of Ypsilanti have something constructive to do when school's out.

"I helped found the Boys and Girls Club because there's no future without children, and the children won't amount to too much or do nearly as well unless they have supervision, education and a chance to develop what God might have given them to begin with," said Bass, one of the founders and a member of the Board of Directors of the Huron Valley Boys and Girls Club.

"They can be endowed very highly with potential IQs, but if it's not developed, not cultured properly by a child's surroundings and family, the child will eventually miss out," he said.

Bass and three other longtime board members will be honored this week when the Boys and Girls Club hosts its first Steak and Burger fund-raising dinner at 7 p.m. Wednesday at the Radisson Resort and Conference Center, 1275 S. Huron.

The club will offer steak to the children and hamburgers to the adults with a special recognition provided to honor Bass, Eugene Beatty and Andrew Smith, both of Ypsilanti, and Dorothy Walker of Pontiac.

"I've known Dr. Bass ever since he's been in town," said Beatty. "He's been our physician for all of that time and I have high respect for him. He's worked hard to get his own youngsters through school and his son and both daughters are outstanding ... They are one of our top families."

Bass said the club was needed in the 1950s, and is still needed today.

"When we started the organization, there were hardly any places in town where youngsters could go, have a good time and still learn something worthwhile," said Bass, who started his family practice in Ypsilanti in 1943.

"Dr. Bass is an outstanding person who's contributed a lot to the community," said Isaac Booker, executive director of the Boys and Girls Club. "I can't

PRESS PHOTO/MARK MUELLER

Bass is a founder and longtime board member of the Huron Valley Boys and Girls Club.

say enough about him."

Bass, 81, said he has no intention of resigning from the board. Nor does he regret the many hours spent at monthly board meetings.

"Absolutely it's been worth it," said

Bass. "I've known many youngsters who were members of the Boys Club and certainly turned out to be worthwhile citizens. I think of family first. My own children went there. My son, Michael, is one. He was 'Boy of the Year' in 1963."

Bass said he wishes more people knew how valuable the club is to the boys and girls who enjoy recreation and educational activities at the facility at 220 N. Park.

"The big problem is we have insufficient funds to bring the organization to where it should be. I'd like to more interest from the whole community," said Bass, adding that he'd like to see the day the club can afford to provide round-trip transportation for young people interested in participating in activities there.

"It seems to me that with the great things the Boys and Girls Club helps a youngster attain," said Bass, "it would be worthwhile getting transportation not only available from the south side, but from the east side, north side and west side. It's a well-founded organization and it certainly keeps them out of the alleys and off the streets."

Bass has hardly limited his community involvement to the Boys and Girls Club. He was one of the founders of the Human Relations Commission of Ypsilanti; founder and past Cubmaster of a Boy Scout Troop at Brown Chapel A.M.E. Church and one of the founders and past president of the Ypsilanti-Ann Arbor Business and Professional League.

This is not to suggest Bass has put a halt to his activities. He is still a member as well as one of the founders of Theta Zeta Lambda, local graduate chapter of Alpha Phi Alpha, the oldest Afro-American Greek Collegiate fraternity; a life member and past president of the Ypsilanti-Willow Run chapter of the National Association for the Advancement of Colored People; one of the founders and president of the Board of Directors of the Parkview Apartments; and founder and member of the Ten-Twenty Investment Club.

His medical career is just as distinguished.

Booker noted that Bass is particularly well-known in the black community because he delivered "practically everybody."

"He delivered just about every black family's babies in the community," said Booker.

Bass is quick to credit his family for supporting him throughout the years.

For information on Wednesday's fund-raiser, call 481-0266.

---

14 0002270948 **DIPLOMA APPLICATION** E 1801

Date 1-3-67

Print Bass / Michael / Thomas

LAST NAME / FIRST NAME / MIDDLE NAME

College or School Education

Degree expected B A

(Give exact title, i.e., B.S. in Chemistry)

When expected? May, 1967

Permanent address from which mail will be forwarded } 77 Greenside

NUMBER AND STREET

Ypsilanti / Michigan 48197

CITY OR TOWN / STATE OR COUNTRY

Expected address next year (if different from permanent address) }

NUMBER AND STREET

CITY OR TOWN / STATE OR COUNTRY

ALUMNI CATALOG CARD

MARRIED WOMEN PLEASE GIVE HUSBAND'S FULL NAME

[The Secretary of this School or College will send this section to the Alumni Catalog Office at once]

(OVER)

Fraternity Honors Physician

MAR 5 1974

An area physician was the recipient recently of the Alpha Phi Alpha, Theta Zeta Lamba chapter, distinguished service award.

Dr. Thomas Bass, at the A Phi A's annual Theta Zeta Lambda alumni chapter dinner dance at Weber's Inn, received the award for "consistent, quiet, compassionate and dedicated contributions to community needs in the best tradition of the Alpha Phi Alpha fraternity."

Presenting the plaque to Dr. Bass, local chapter president Milton Brown said, he is "a physician who has healed not only individuals but also the wounds of a community caused by the stress and strain of growth and development. For 41 years, this is a true Alpha who we honor tonight."

Dr. Bass was born in Paterson, N.J. He received his AB degree from Lincoln University in Pennsylvania and his medical degree from Meharry Medical College. Dr. Bass also received his masters in public health from the U. M.

He has three children, one of whom, his son Michael, played football for U-M.

Dr. Bass is a member of the American Medical Association, the National Medical Association and the Washtenaw County Medical Society.

He resides with his wife, Louise, in Ypsilanti.

NEWS PHOTO • COLLEEN FITZGERALD

Louise 'Ma' Bass, 70, retired from East Middle School in 1985. Now, pupils go to her west side home to partake of her knowledge. And reading and math aren't the only subjects. 'We get around to talking about such things as how long to stay on the telephone without riling your parents, disagreements with mom or dad, boy-girl relationships,' Bass says.

APR 23 1993

Retired 'Ma Bass' keeps teaching from book-crammed Ypsilanti home

By ROBERT L. ROMAKER
NEWS STAFF REPORTER

YPSILANTI — Louise Bass has so many youngsters coming in and out of her house that "the neighbors tell me that if they didn't know better, they'd think I'm running a crack house."

Bass, 70, retired from East Middle School in 1985. But the teaching — now informal and unpaid — continues from her brick home on the city's west side.

Bass keeps a notebook, blocked into time periods, which lists appointments with youngsters, who come to her with their academic problems.

Seated in her wheelchair, she apologizes for the lived-in look of her home. "I don't like housework," she confides, "but when people see all these papers and books and know that I use them to tutor kids, they excuse me for the messed-up look."

Books line several shelves of the living and dining rooms. There are more in the basement. "We've always been suckers for books," Bass admits. There used to be a rule around here that you don't go to bed or to the bathroom without a book."

Circulatory system problems, which Bass developed about 10 years ago, slowed but didn't stop her; she completed the last six years of her formal teaching career in a wheelchair.

"The boys in my classes used to compete among themselves to see who could be my pusher," she laughs.

She also was known at the

school as "Ma Bass," according to principal Harold Lounsberry, because of "a motherly willingness to help students and staff." Lounsberry adds that "she wasn't afraid to get after anybody who did something wrong — from student to principal."

Now students come to her home, some referred by people who knew her at East Middle, others referred by youngsters helped previously by "Ma Bass."

They learn more than reading and math. "We get around to talking about such things as how long to stay on the telephone without riling your parents, disagreements with mom or dad, boy-girl relationships," Bass says.

The importance of education was always stressed in the Bass home. Bass and her husband, Thomas, a retired physician, saw all three of their children graduate from Ypsilanti High School. Their daughters, Leah and Ann, earned master's degrees and now work in professional fields.

Their son, Michael, served as president of his senior class at Ypsilanti High, made all-state in football, earned a scholarship to the University of Michigan and played football professionally, most notably with the Washington Redskins. Currently, he manages a resort in the Bahamas.

As a defensive back for the Redskins, Michael was involved in one of pro football's most bizarre plays. Washington was playing Miami in the 1973 Super

ROMAKER AT LARGE

Bowl. Miami kicker Garo Ypremenian was ready to try a field goal. There was a problem with the snap and a befuddled Ypremenian, fleeing oncoming tacklers, lobbed a crippled pass at nobody in particular. Bass flashed in, picked off the wobbler and raced 49 yards for Washington's lone touchdown. But, Miami won the game, 14-7.

"Up until Michael intercepted the pass, I was wondering what to tell my friends about the game," says Bass, "because the Redskins played lousy."

A graduate of Hampton Institute in Hampton, Va., Bass started her teaching career at Newport News, Va., before moving to Michigan in 1942. Her tenure in the Ypsilanti school system covered 29 years.

In "retirement" she's still prominent in the Ypsilanti Association of Women's Clubs, senior citizen groups and other civic organizations. But providing help and counsel to youngsters still dominates her life. She frowns when asked why.

"What else would I do?" she challenges. "There isn't anything to take the place of working with kids."

'Humbling' honor

Ypsilanti native, ex-Washington Redskin Bass feted by team

BY RICH REZLER
News Sports Reporter

Ypsilanti native Mike Bass, already responsible for one of the more memorable moments in Super Bowl history, is now listed among the greatest Washington Redskins of all-time.

A former all-state football player at Ypsilanti High School and a two-year starter at the University of Michigan, Bass said he's flattered to be one of 70 coaches and players honored with that title in conjunction with the team's 70th anniversary celebration.

"I had never really won anything in professional football before, so this is really the first honor I received," said Bass, a starting cornerback for the Redskins from 1969-75.

"I heard that they were coming out with this list, but I never thought that I would be one of those selected," he added.

His 1972-73 Washington team came close to winning Super Bowl VII, losing, 14-7, to the Miami Dolphins, whose 17-0 record remains the NFL's only unbeaten season. The Redskins' only points came with 2:07 remaining in the game when kicker Garo Yepremian picked up a fumbled field goal attempt and awkwardly passed the ball. Bass picked the loose ball out of the air and returned it 49 yards for a touchdown.

"It happened so quickly," Bass said of the play. "It really was a tribute to coach (George) Allen for his dedication to detail. My job was to get the ball if it's blocked."

That play was one of many memories discussed with former teammates and other Redskin greats during a weekend-long celebration last month that included on-field introductions at the Redskins' game against the Colts.

"The whole affair at halftime was fabulous," Bass said. "When we walked out of the tunnel at the end of second quarter, the fans actually ignored the game to applaud us. Even the players on the bench turned around and applauded us.

"It was very humbling to be among some of those great, great players. It was a great weekend. They treated us like kings."

After graduating from Ypsilanti in 1963, Bass was part of the Wolverines' 1964 team that beat Oregon in the Rose Bowl and finished No. 4 in both the AP and UPI polls. He then started at cornerback for the 1965 and 1966 teams.

He was drafted by the Green Bay Packers, coached by legendary Vince Lombardi, and was the team's final cut. He then spent two seasons on the Detroit Lions taxi squad, where Bass says now he "was never really given an opportunity."

When Bass was cut by Green Bay, Lombardi told him he had a future in the NFL. That stellar future began when Lombardi took over the Redskins and brought Bass with him.

"After wasting two years, quite frankly I was really lucky when coach Lombardi came to Washington," Bass said. "He had told me not to give up, and I didn't."

After retiring from the NFL, Bass moved to the Bahamas and raised two daughters while operating a resort. He accepted his current position with the University of Florida's office of academic support five years ago so his daughters could experience life in the United States.

While Bass admits he isn't able to return to the Ypsilanti area often, he still cherishes fond memories.

"I don't have family there anymore, but there's lots of quasi-family and kids that I went to school with," Bass said. "I'm still very close to all of them. There's still a lot of things that always remind me of the old Ypsi High."

Rich Rezler can be reached at (734) 994-6812, or rrezler@annarbornews.com.

SPECIAL TO THE NEWS PHOTO
Mike Bass was an all-state selection at Ypsilanti High School and was a two-year starter for the University of Michigan. He played in the NFL from 1969-75.

Ypsilanti doctor, wife honored by hundreds

Dr. and Mrs. Bass are honored by community

SUNDAY DEC 9 1979

YPSILANTI — It started out to be a small affair — but it grew until some 400 people turned out Saturday night to honor Dr. Thomas Bass and his wife Louise for "what they've done for the community."

A young boy is guided out of trouble . . . a small injustice because of prejudice is corrected . . . a body is healed . . . a little girl is helped to learn to read when others thought she could not . . .

Scores of such achievements that have helped hundreds are the reason that big, grateful crowd turned out for an appreciation banquet at the Hoyt Conference Center on the campus of Eastern Michigan Campus.

IT WAS NOT a black tie affair. It was just people coming out on a cold night to convey warm, informal appreciation to a couple they treasure.

As Doris Clay, one of the banquet organizers, put it, "We just wanted to tell them how much we love them, tell 'em we care about what they've done for them, tell 'em we care about what they've done for the community. I can't list all the activities they been involved in but they sure have done some work."

It started in 1943. Thomas J. Bass, of Patterson, N.J., was by then a doctor, having gained honors along the way from Lincoln University and Meharry Medical College and then interning at the Freedman's Hospital in Washington D.C. In October of that year, he started his medical practice in Ypsilanti.

Although he was busy as most doctors are, he found time for community projects, too. The list is long: Boy Scouts; active membership in the Brown Chapel A.M.E. Church, the National Association of Colored People and Ypsilanti Human Relations Commission. He was former chief of the medical staff of Beyer Memorial Hospital.

There is lots more, but you get the idea.

And, equally, Louise Bass has left her mark. She was raised in Dayton, Ohio, she went on to Hampton Institute in Hampton Va. for her bachelor's degree and completed graduate work at EMU and the University of Michigan.

Currently, she teaches math at the East Middle School and is director of the mathematics instruction center there.

SHE IS a member of the Board of Directors, National Association of Colored Women's Clubs and president of the Ypsilanti Association of Women's Clubs.

In 1976, Mrs. Bass received from the National Council of Negro Women, its Leadership and Community Involvement Award and later the Humanitarian Award from the Ypsilanti-Ann Arbor Business and Professional League.

Last night the tributes for that kind of work came to both of them. Their marks run deep and will always be felt. That's why so many people showed up to say, "Thanks."

[Registrar's Office]   UNIVERSITY OF MICHIGAN, 1943   Encircle one

(FALL) SPR SUM 8 WK

Print Name Thomas James Bass

FR SO JR SR (GRAD) SPEC

ALL SENIOR AND GRADUATE STUDENTS: This office cannot check your record for graduation unless you give full name of degree and or certificate and date when expected.

Fall Term 1943

P.H.

DEGREE Master Public Health CERT. DATE 1944, June

DEPARTMENT { e.g., Drawing, Piano, English, Epidemiology.	No. of Course	Hrs. of Credit	Grade	Place and Time			Instructor
				Room & Bldg.	Days	Hour	
Epidemiology	200	2					
Epidemiology	202	2					
Pub. Health Practice	201	2					
Pub. Health Practice	202	1					
Pub. Health Practice	204	2					
Pub. Health Practice	210	2					
Environ. Health	200	2					
Environ. Health	202	2					
Environ. Health	241	2					

STUDENT: Do not fill in Place and Time until these courses have been properly approved in the classification room.

Elections Approved _____

[Registrar's Office]   UNIVERSITY OF MICHIGAN, 1944   Encircle one

FALL (SPR) SUM 8 WK

Print Name Thos. J. Bass

FR SO JR SR (GRAD) SPEC

ALL SENIOR AND GRADUATE STUDENTS: This office cannot check your record for graduation unless you give full name of degree and or certificate and date when expected.

Spring Term 1944

P.H.

DEGREE M.P.H. CERT. DATE June 1944

DEPARTMENT { e.g., Drawing, Piano, English, Epidemiology.	No. of Course	Hrs. of Credit	Grade	Place and Time			Instructor
				Room & Bldg.	Days	Hour	
Epidemiology	241	6		N. Kieffer & Pub. H.	M.w.Th		
Epidemiology	255	2		Pub. H	F	9-12	
Epidemiology	257	3		Pub. H	F	1-4	
PHP	203	2		Pub. H	T; Th	1	
PHP	205	2					
PHP	245	1			W & f	9	
PHYSICAL ED. EXEMPT							
P.H.P.	220	2					

STUDENT: Do not fill in Place and Time until these courses have been properly approved in the classification room.

Elections Approved _____

THE JEWETT FAMILY

Jewett Family Narrative

GEORGE HENRY JEWETT THE FIRST was a blacksmith. He did well in his profession from what I've been told. I've never seen a photo of him, but he is our eldest family member that we know of and can trace our history to.

He and his wife had a son and a daughter, George Jewett II and Leticia Jewett, whom we called "Aunt Letty." George Jewett II became the first Black man to play football for the University of Michigan and Northwestern University. Aunt Letty had no children and lived past the age of 90. George Jewett II would graduate with his degree in medicine from Northwestern, having attended both U of M and Northwestern. He would eventually return to Ann Arbor to open his own cleaning and pressing shop called The Valet. Suddenly, at the young age of 38, George passed away while working at his shop.

Due to the fact that George was the first Black football player to attend both universities and compete in the Big Ten Conference, in 2021 a trophy was created in his honor. The two teams will compete for the trophy whenever they play each other in the future.

George Jewett II had two sons, Richard and George III, whom we called "Uncle Bill." Richard married Iva May Dean. They had 3 children: Ruth, Iva Lillian, and Coleman. Coleman and Yvonne Jewett are my parents, as well as my brother Michael's.

Coleman had a long, successful career in education. During his tenure, he worked as a counselor, a teacher consultant, and most notably, a middle school administrator. The bulk of his career was spent as an administrator at Tappan Middle School in Ann Arbor. Coleman was also an entrepreneur like his grandfather. He sold his handmade wood crafts at the Ann Arbor Farmer's Market for over 40 years. When he passed away in January 2013 at the age of 78, his former (now adult) students and many others had a set of his Adirondack chairs bronzed. The chairs are now a permanent fixture at the Farmer's Market.

Yvonne Jewett was me and Mike's mom. She was a secretary at Mack Elementary School for a long time before working at the Ann Arbor Public Schools administration building. While a secretary, she made it a point to learn all the names of the students in kindergarten. If the student remained at Mack from kindergarten through sixth grade, she would know all the students' names. She and Coleman married in 1956, I was born in 1958, and Michael in 1960.

This local family history makes my brother Michael Jewett and I 5th generation Ann Arborites. Growing up, we lived in Cornell Courts, which was married student housing at Eastern Michigan University. My parents were married when my father attended classes there. From there, we moved to 856 Wickfield Court. Wickfield Court is one block north of A2 STEAM. At that time it was called Northside School, and it was kindergarten through sixth grade.

After that, we lived at Longshore Apartments. Then we moved to 1415 Pontiac Trail. Our Pontiac Trail address was next door to the Beckley House, a large, yellow brick building that was part of the Underground Railroad. We lived there until I graduated from Huron High School and left home to attend classes at Michigan State University.

My brother Michael Jewett has had a long career as a radio announcer for WEMU. He's always educated himself on the careers of blues and jazz artists the most. He's been working with the WEMU crew since 1984. The station has most recently won an award for Outstanding Broadcasting.

I have worked in education off and on since 1974. The "off time" has been spent attending college classes and working in other fields i.e., home building, graphic design, and test driving cars for Chrysler.

So if I get asked where I'm from, my answer is: My family has been here since 1856. We've been here a long time.

Submitted by Michele Jewett Trigg

The Jewett Family

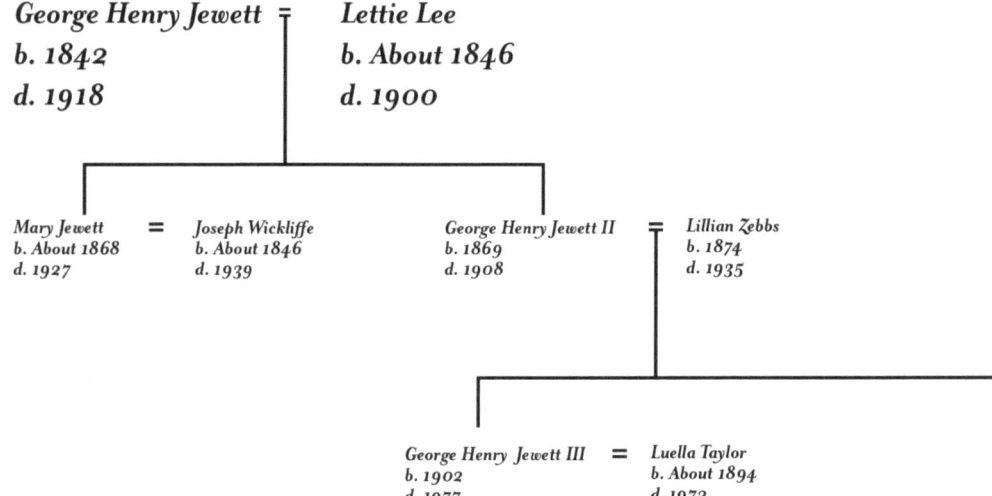

George Henry Jewett
b. 1842
d. 1918

Lettie Lee
b. About 1846
d. 1900

Mary Jewett
b. About 1868
d. 1927

= Joseph Wickliffe
b. About 1846
d. 1939

George Henry Jewett II
b. 1869
d. 1908

= Lillian Zebbs
b. 1874
d. 1935

George Henry Jewett III
b. 1902
d. 1977

= Luella Taylor
b. About 1894
d. 1972

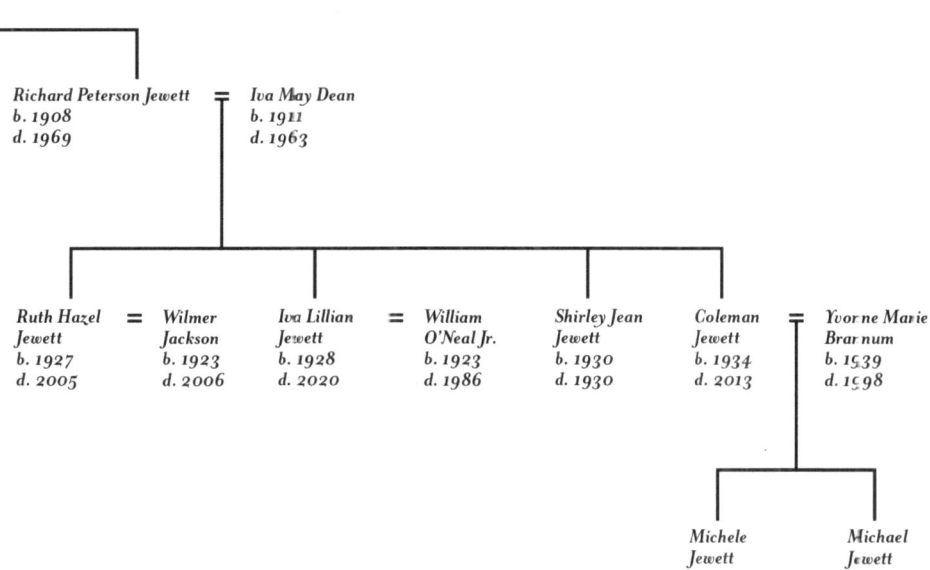

Richard Peterson Jewett = Iva May Dean
b. 1908   b. 1911
d. 1969   d. 1963

Ruth Hazel = Wilmer   Iva Lillian = William   Shirley Jean   Coleman = Yvonne Marie
Jewett   Jackson   Jewett   O'Neal Jr.   Jewett   Jewett   Brannum
b. 1927   b. 1923   b. 1928   b. 1923   b. 1930   b. 1934   b. 1939
d. 2005   d. 2006   d. 2020   d. 1986   d. 1930   d. 2013   d. 1998

Michele   Michael
Jewett   Jewett

Interview with Michele Jewett Trigg

MICHELE JEWETT TRIGG: Hello, my name is Michele Jewett Trigg. I'm a descendant of George Henry Jewett I. My father is the late Coleman Jewett, which many people know.

JOYCE HUNTER: Thank you, Michele, for participating and for doing this interview. I'm going to start with the questions, we have four. The first one is: can you describe your family tree and ancestry?

MICHELE JEWETT TRIGG: Yes, thank you. My great-great-grandfather was George Jewett I. He migrated from Bowling Green, Kentucky, in 1856. He came here and had two children, George Henry Jewett II and his brother George Henry Jewett III. My great grandfather was the first Black football player for the University of Michigan as well. He also became the first Black football player for Northwestern University and the Big Ten Championship. They now have a trophy to honor him. George Jewett, the football player, was my grandfather. His father Richard was my great-grandfather's son and Coleman's dad. Coleman and Yvonne Jewett had two children, which I am the first born of Coleman and Yvonne Jewett. It goes: George Henry Jewett I, George Henry Jewett II, then he had George Henry Jewett III and Richard Jewett, which is Coleman Jewett's father, my father and great-grandfather. All of that side of my family would be considered of African-American descent. On Coleman's mom's side, our great-grandfather was Native American. His name was Alfred Dean, and he was a Delaware Native American. That's where some of my lineage has transpired over the years as well.

My father Coleman Jewett was very well-known, of course, here in Ann Arbor. He was an administrator at Tappan Junior High for many years and had a lot of students who respected and admired him. As a result, they've created a set of bronze Adirondack chairs at the Ann Arbor Farmers Market because that's where he was a vendor for over 47 years. To my knowledge, my brother and I—Michael and I—are the only two people in this area of African-American descent who have two monuments, or artifacts maybe you could say, in our people's honor. That being the bronze chairs at the Ann Arbor market, and the George Jewett trophy, now in the possession of the University of Michigan.

JOYCE HUNTER: I'm going to go to question two, and you might have touched on that already. How did your family arrive in the Ann Arbor / Ypsilanti / Washtenaw County area?

MICHELE JEWETT TRIGG: George Jewett I was the blacksmith. He came here from Bowling Green, Kentucky, as I said. His motivations, I have never gotten the total story on that, but I would think because his skill, his craft enabled him to make a pretty good living here. Like many African-Americans, I think he came here because he saw the opportunity to create a better life for himself through his skill, his craft. It's interesting to me because my father also developed craft and became an entrepreneur. We have this theme in my family, on my father's side, being not only having a job working for the corporation, if you will, but also becoming entrepreneurs. My father, my great-grandfather, who had his own business called The Valet on the corner of Williams and South State Street, that's where his dry cleaning business took place. He was also an entrepreneur, and then George Henry Jewett I had his own business as a blacksmith, so he, too, was an entrepreneur. We came here through George Henry Jewett I because of his crafts and his gifts of being able to make a good life for himself here.

JOYCE HUNTER: We're going to go to question three. Were there any local places of importance for your family? If so, please describe the place and why it was important to your ancestors.

MICHELE JEWETT TRIGG: Well, the first thing that comes to mind, actually, is through my father's work when in the summertime he was a supervisor at West Park. At that time in Ann Arbor, there were many African-American families that lived on the west side of Ann Arbor, and my father used to do his woodworking there. He brought all his saws and stuff like that there and did it there. They had a wading pool at the time, I remember watching him go start the wading pool and then go walk off and do a bunch of other stuff and come back and turn the water off later, so people came down to the West Park and we played tetherball, we played this game called box hockey. We had a hockey box, so the puck would never leave the box unless you popped it out too hard. The French Dukes used to come down to the market and practice their steps at West Park. My father used to run baseball games. They had two baseball diamonds down there at the time. We had a baseball team going, and I would sit and watch him write down all the names of the players and everybody coming up to bat. West Park was actually one of the places that has special meaning to my family. Another place I would say is we claim Jewett Avenue here in Ann Arbor, which is off the South Industrial / Packard area. My father said it wasn't named after our family, but we're the only people we know still here, so we claim it as ours anyway. That's a special thing to us. Of course, the trophies that have been made in my great-grandfather's honor now at U-M, and my father's chairs at the Ann Arbor Farmers Market. Who could ask me for more? We have two pieces of things that can go into eternity in my family name. All of those things are very special to my family.

JOYCE HUNTER: Tell me where you lived when you were growing up. That wasn't the question, but I'd like to know more about that.

MICHELE JEWETT TRIGG: The time when my father was actually a student at Eastern Michigan, we lived in Cornell Apartments because he was married, so he lived in married student housing on EMU Campus. And then 856 Wickfield Court. If I ever do a memoir, I'll put that address in there. But that was our childhood home, my brother and I, our childhood home. On the Northside, walking distance from Northside School, which they now call STEAM, it was in a court,

Wickfield Court, and there were other Black families that lived on that court. Blackwell, Franklin, just to name a few. That is where we spent some of my time growing up. We lived in Longshore Apartments for a while when my dad was taking college classes and then we got a two family home on Pontiac Trail. That put us next door to what's called the Beckley House, which is on the corner of Pontiac Trail and Argo. It was part of the Underground Railroad, so we lived next door to the Beckley House. When we lived at 1415 Pontiac, we lived next door to a historical home in Ann Arbor, and we lived there until I graduated from high school and went away to college.

JOYCE HUNTER: Thank you. The fourth question.

MICHELE JEWETT TRIGG: Yes.

JOYCE HUNTER: You already talked about some of these, but if you want to add or repeat, are there any people, artifacts, or pictures unique to your family that you would like to share?

MICHELE JEWETT TRIGG: The people I would like to acknowledge or say thank you to definitely, Rita and Peter Heydon of the Mosaic Foundation. Thank you for your gifts to my father's project at the Ann Arbor Farmers Market. All the people who put money, time, and effort into creating my father's Adirondack chairs at the Farmers Market, thank you. His students. Many students, I can't even name or know all of them. Thank you for your time and effort towards my father's memorial project at the Ann Arbor Farmers Market. Warde Manuel. The sports director of the University of Michigan, thank you for spearheading a project to honor the first Black football player at U-M. Thank you for that. All the people at U-M and Northwestern who helped out creating that trophy in my great-grandfather's honor. Those are just a few of the people I would like to thank. O'Neal Construction Company for seeing to it that my father's chairs made it to the property at the Ann Arbor Farmers Market near his boots. Thank you for that. I should have wrote all the names down, but it's a long list, but that's just a short list of the people and all of the things that I am grateful for and my family is grateful for that have been created in my family honor. I have a few pictures. This is a very common photo, actually, of George Jewett, which has already been recorded and posted through your website. There's plenty of pictures of Coleman as well. I have a sample of Coleman's chair, one of his little mini-chairs that he did at the Ann Arbor Farmers Market.

JOYCE HUNTER: I actually have a couple pieces of his work that I purchased from him.

MICHELE JEWETT TRIGG: Yes, I've met many people just in my goings and comings from home where they have pieces of his work too. Since his passing, some people have re-inherited some to me, I'm grateful for.

JOYCE HUNTER: Those are the four questions, and so I want to thank you for doing the interview and for participating in this exhibit. Unless you have any final thing you want to share, I'm going to have Heidi stop the recording.

George Jewett II

*(Left to right) George Jewett II,
Coleman Jewett, Richard Jewett,
Michele and Michael Jewett*

Lillian Zebbs Jewett

U-M 1892-1893 varsity football team with George Jewett II

Jewett family photos

Family at the U–M vs. Northwestern game in October 2021, the first time the two teams played for the George Jewett Trophy.

Hazel Derrick, Russel Derrick, and Coleman Jewett on his mom Iva May Jewett's lap

Left to right: siblings Iva Lillian, Coleman, and Ruth Jewett

Michele and Michael Jewett

Coleman Jewett married Yvonne Brannum, 1957

Iva May Jewett   *Yvonne Jewett*

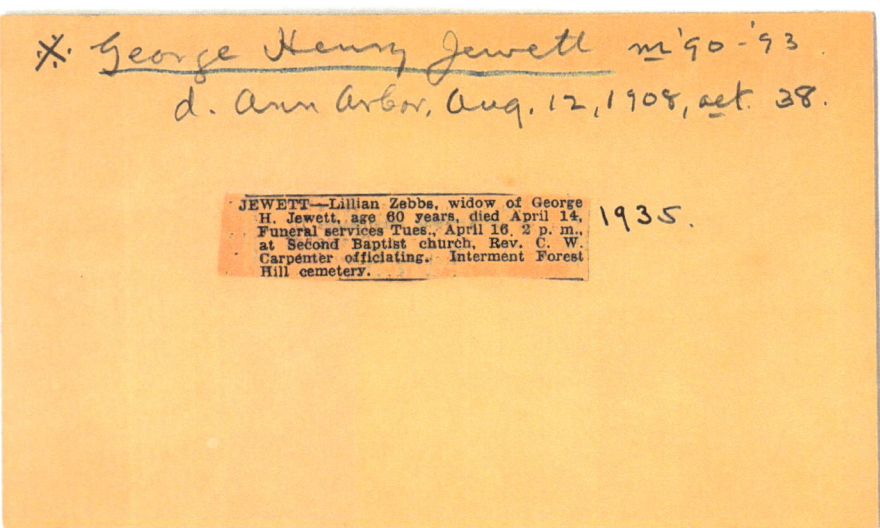

Tenney, Sherman, Bentley & Guthrie
Law Offices
120 South LaSalle Street
Chicago 3, Illinois

January 19, 1955

Mr. T. Hawley Tapping, General Secretary
Alumni Association
Alumni Memorial Hall
Ann Arbor, Michigan

Dear Tap:

In further answer to your letter of the 7th Inst. relative to George Jewett. In my letter to you of the 14th, I told you that I had some information about him that I would be glad to give you - so here goes: George Jewett played on the Michigan Varsity team in the fall of 1890. I think he played in every game during that season. Unless I am mistaken, he was born in Ann Arbor and lived there with his mother. He played on his local high school team. He matriculated in the Class of 1894, Literary Department. He was very modest and retiring, an extremely fast runner and had the gift of being able to run through a broken field like the "Galloping Ghost", Red Grange, of later days. He undoubtedly was the best player on the Michigan team of 1890.

Aside from my very pleasant acquaintance with him, two experiences relating to him fix him very clearly in my mind. When we played Albion College at Albion, Michigan, in the fall of 1890, his presence was resented by both the Albion team and the spectators. Every effort was made to get him ruled off and traps were set for him to bring this about. On one occasion he was charged with "slugging" and the cry went up from the crowd to "Kill the 'nigger'". The crowd surged out on the field, blows were struck and a riot was in the making when the local police intervened and the game went on with Jewett still in the line-up.

On another occasion when the team was obliged to stay overnight in Indianapolis the clerk in the only available hotel there refused to let Jewett register. Of course the other members of the team backed him up, as well as some local alumni, and he stayed with the other members of the team at the hotel.

According to my best recollection, for two years after the 1890 season, Jewett was not seen on the Michigan campus or football field. In the fall of 1893 he surprised everybody by

Tenney, Sherman, Bentley & Guthrie

Mr. T. Hawley Tapping   Page Two   January 19, 1955

appearing on the Northwestern University team that played Michigan on November 18 of that year. Northwestern was supposed to have a very good eleven that season. It was coached by Paul Noyes (then in the law school at Northwestern), brilliant full-back at Yale the year before. He played that position in the Michigan game. The Northwestern players and rooters came to Ann Arbor on a special train with all kinds of money to bet on their team. Most, or all of this, was snapped up when they arrived in Ann Arbor. During the first five minutes of play Jewett got the ball, ran through the entire Michigan team and scored a touchdown. Northwestern 6 - Michigan 0. Many bets were doubled. The final score was Michigan 72 - Northwestern 6. Look it up in the official records.

As to whether or not Jewett was the first colored man to play on a University football team, I am not informed. How-ever, for about ten years, beginning with the year 1898, I followed football very closely as player, coach, official and reporter for Chicago newspapers and I never heard of a negro playing on any team, University or otherwise. There was a dark skinned South Sea Islander on the Oberlin team when they played Michigan at Ann Arbor in 1890, I think it was. He was a stocky, fierce-looking fellow with flashing black eyes and was a tough player. The Michigan rooters wasted no time in dubbing him "The Cannibal". In the early Nineties there was a colored man on the Harvard Varsity team who afterwards became Attorney General of the State of Massachusetts.

Whatever became of Jewett after his appearance in the fall of 1893, I do not know. You inquire in your letter why he did not receive a letter; the answer is that at that time there wasn't any such animal. Every man scratched up his own football outfit. The pants I wore originally belonged to "Snake" Ames, Princeton football great of the '89 team. At Michigan not even a sweater was handed out. In those days we wore canvas jackets and if a man played on the team, he took a lead pencil, ink or charcoal and put a letter "M" on his jacket. In the pictures I am sending you, you will see that Jewett is rigged out in this way. There was no awarding of letters and the squads were then so small that there was no discussion as to who was or was not entitled to wear a lettered jacket. We practiced in a corner of the campus near where the Waterman Gymnasium now stands. There was no grass on the field - just sand, gravel and larger stones. We played our games on the old fair grounds with large

Tenney, Sherman, Bentley & Guthrie

Mr. T. Hawley Tapping   Page Three   January 19, 1955

boulders sticking up here and there above the surface of the
ground. When we played Chicago University in Chicago, the
spectators stood behind ropes tied to sticks stuck into the
ground a few feet back from the lines of the playing field and
a hat was passed around to defray expenses.

Under separate cover I am sending you a picture of the
team as it played in the fall of 1890 and a picture of 1894 Class
team of the same year. You will see Jewett's picture in both
of these. Do not be misled by the '91 on the football in the
Varsity Team picture. This figure was used, no doubt, because
Malley, the captain, and others in the picture belonged to the
class of 1891. Of course, the football should have been marked
'90 instead of '91.

You will also observe that there was another colored
man who played on the '94 team. This was R. A. J. Shaw, a
gentlemanly, scholarly fellow who played good football. He was
quickly dubbed "Alphabetical Shaw".

It occurs to me that duplicates of the pictures I am
sending you may be available to you. If so, you may want to
return my copies to me and I will hand them down to one of my
grandsons who is now playing prep football in preparation, I
hope, for playing at Michigan someday. If the keeper of the
athletic archives at Michigan feels these pictures are of
sufficient interest to be retained and framed, I will be delighted
to have them appropriately framed and will gladly defray any
expense in this connection. There is enclosed, for use with
these pictures, separate slips showing the names of the players
on the two teams in question.

I have had a very good time recalling to mind the early
football days at Michigan. This I did in order to write something
that is even halfway intelligent. In any event, I hope it serves
your purpose. In this connection don't forget what Mark Twain
said when asked in his later years if he didn't have difficulty
in recalling events that happened way back in his boyhood days.
He replied that he could remember quite easily and clearly not
only the things that happened then but many things that never
happened at all!

Tenney, Sherman, Bentley & Guthrie

Mr. T. Hawley Tapping   Page Four   January 19, 1955

          I was delighted to hear, through you, of Ralph Stone
after so many years of "no-see". Please give him my very best
regards. The enclosed copy of this letter is intended for
him.

          With sincere personal regards, I am

                              Very truly yours,

                                        Roger Sherman.

RS/ew
Encl.
P. S. Later -

          Yours of the 18th Inst. just received. Sorry I won't
see you next week in Chicago but I am taking a train tomorrow
morning for Florida.

                         R. S.

THE MICHIGAN ALUMNUS *Quarterly Review*

UNIVERSITY OF MICHIGAN, ANN ARBOR
4010 Administration

ROUTING
REFERRED TO
TAPPING

MONEY
MORGAN
WILSON
McLOUTH
RUSSELL
EDITORIAL
A. C. O.

January 6, 1955

Mr. T. Hawley Tapping
Alumni Memorial Hall
Campus

Dear Tap:

Bob Morgan suggested that I send you the following paragraph from a letter written by Ralph Stone to
Charlie Sink under date of December 27, 1954:

"George Jewett--I remember George very distinct-
ly. Today, sports writers mention 'so and so' as the
<u>first</u> negro on a college football squad. If any
negro was first, it was George. I was on the Michigan
squad with him in the fall of 1890. George was a
'star' in his own right. Without benefit of blockers
to clear a path for him, he could dodge, wriggle,
twist, pivot and whirl through the opposing team as
well as the modern No. 1 All American back could do
with the help of a mighty bulk of human flesh to
block for him."

The rest of the letter refers to other parts of
Charlie's article in the last number of the <u>Quarterly
Review</u>.

Sincerely yours,

Frank E. Robbins
Editor

FER/eem

The University Musical Society
of the
University of Michigan
Burton Memorial Tower, Ann Arbor

OFFICES OF
CHARLES A. SINK,
PRESIDENT
THOR JOHNSON,
GUEST CONDUCTOR
LESTER McCOY,
ASSOCIATE CONDUCTOR

CHORAL UNION CONCERTS
MAY FESTIVAL CONCERTS
CHAMBER MUSIC FESTIVAL
EXTRA CONCERT SERIES
MESSIAH CONCERTS

January 7, 1955

ROUTING

MONEY, AMOUNT _____
REFERRED TO
TAPPING
MORGAN _____
FINLAYSON _____
McLOUTH _____
RUSSELL _____
EDITORIAL _____
A.C.O.

Tap — for your information FER

Dr. Frank E. Robbins,
4010 Administration Bldg.,
Ann Arbor, Michigan.

Dear Frank:

In further reference to the George Jewett
matter, may I mention that so far as I remember
he had two sons, who were little shavers in the
days when I knew the father. I note in the
telephone book the names of George H. Jewett,
503 N. 4th Avenue, phone No. 2-3919; and that of
Richard P. Jewett, 209 E. Kingsley, phone No.
3-4956.

I have no doubt but that these two men are
his two sons, and you might like to get in
touch with them to see what they can tell you
about their father's student days. Undoubtedly
he must have told them many stories of his
football prowess.

Very cordially yours,

Charles

CAS:MF

THE KERSEY FAMILY

Kersey Family Narrative

TO DESCRIBE OUR KERSEY FAMILY lineage here in Washtenaw County, Michigan, we must take a glimpse at our past generations. It began in Ypsilanti in the decade of the 1880s with John Kersey (1847-1897) born in Noblesville, Indiana. His children would settle in Michigan, making Ypsilanti their home. Elisha Kersey farmed in the area now known as Crosley Wildlife and Fishery in Jennings County, Indiana. Elisha was born circa 1824 in Georgia, and social conditions suggest that Elisha's ancestors were of mixture of First Nations, Black, and white. In the late 16th century, our family's racial designation in early U.S. Census records were: "mulatto" and "free people of color."

The early generations of Kerseys settled in the areas of Elbert and Wilkes County in eastern Georgia. After the war of 1812, large tracts of land became available for purchase due to the aftermath of Britain's defeat on American soil. Further investigation on Census records and research finds a large colonial American presence of the Kerseys in 17th Century Virginia.

We bring our attention to the generation of Elisha, his wife Mary (Philips) Kersey and children, who settled in Indiana in the 1840s. This timeline is crucial considering the complexity of the Underground Railroad and social issues in America at that time. During this decade, the Kersey family settled in eastern Indiana, near the Ohio River, at its Kentucky border. We have researched that they were involved in helping runaway slaves through the networking of their farms, properties, and churches going into the northern cities throughout the central terminus of Indiana, Michigan, and eventually to Canada. The disappointment of such loss of properties and the value of land stemming from unfair treatment could not be counted out. Community life in the African-American experience involved the spirituality and connecting of the churches. Our family records revealed that Stephen and Sally Kersey sold property to the Richland African Methodist Episcopal Church on December 17, 1841. This congregation would help runaway slaves through its network and had involvement in the Underground Railroad system into the 1850s and beyond.

To further elaborate, the Underground Railroad stations from Indiana to Canada were crucial in our family's migration, and here's why. Beginning in 1850, the Fugitive Slave Act was enforced, threatening people of color regardless of their "free persons of color" and Indian status. This movement of Kerseys in Terre Haute, a city in western Indiana, led a migration to central Michigan from Battle Creek to Detroit. The 1850 Census shows the extended Kersey families in areas such as Vernon Township, Indiana, and Noblesville, near Indianapolis, were their concentrated settlements. Alexander and Elisha, who were brothers, moved their families through Kalamazoo, then to Canada. In the early 1850s, Colchester, North Buxton, and finally Dresden, Ontario, were the ending points of the Underground Railroad connections.

It's interesting to note that the properties where the Kerseys lived in the U.S. involved the Quakers help to aid fugitives to freedom. Ultimately freedom came to the wandering travelers into the Canadian cities of Sandwich (now Windsor), Amhurstburg, Chatham, Dresden, and Owen Sound, Ontario. There was a need for gifted and skilled carpenters and brick masons to assist new communities of refugees escaping the United States. The call to Dresden was made by Reverend Josiah Henson, whom the Kersey family helped to establish a manumission school called "Dawn," a settlement for fugitive slaves building a new life in Canada. On July 30th, 2023, a momentous celebration convened, renaming the former home of Rev. Henson the "Josiah Henson Museum for African-Canadian History" in Dresden, Ontario.

Finally, where John Kersey settled in Washtenaw County, Michigan, in 1882 or 1883, at the height of a booming industrial enterprise of various trades, such as grain and flour manufacturing. Soaps, mineral salts, grist mills, paper mills, and a health sanitarium attracted many to

Ypsilanti from around the country. Shortly after John established his new home in Ypsilanti, the tragedy of two children's early deaths struck his family, and on July 3, 1897, he passed away at fifty years old.

Post-Underground Railroad families migrated back into Washtenaw County, Michigan, from Canada after the 1863 Emancipation Proclamation was declared. The roots of many African-American families would and did make Washtenaw County and Ypsilanti the Black Paris of the Midwest. We know and have documented ten Kersey generations that would call this place home.

Compiled by Rev. Terrence A. Vick

The Kersey Family

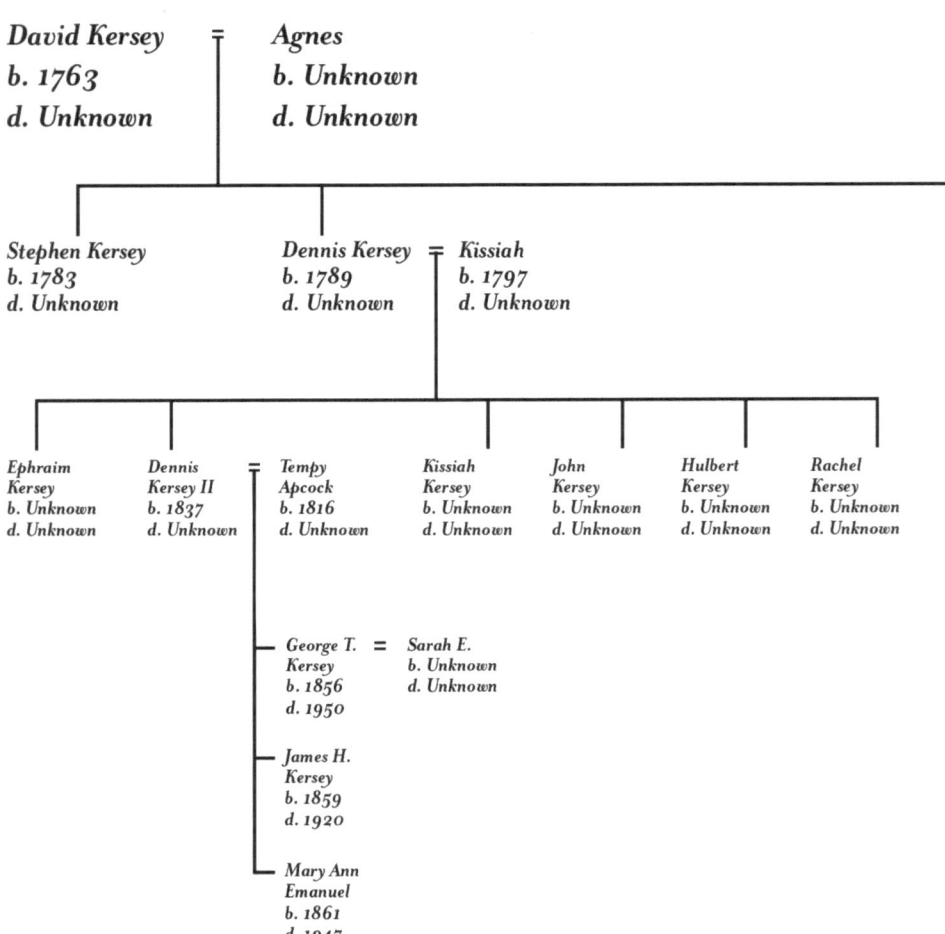

David Kersey
b. 1763
d. Unknown

Agnes
b. Unknown
d. Unknown

Stephen Kersey
b. 1783
d. Unknown

Dennis Kersey
b. 1789
d. Unknown

Kissiah
b. 1797
d. Unknown

**Ephraim
Kersey**
b. Unknown
d. Unknown

**Dennis
Kersey II**
b. 1837
d. Unknown

**Tempy
Apcock**
b. 1816
d. Unknown

**Kissiah
Kersey**
b. Unknown
d. Unknown

**John
Kersey**
b. Unknown
d. Unknown

**Hulbert
Kersey**
b. Unknown
d. Unknown

**Rachel
Kersey**
b. Unknown
d. Unknown

*George T.
Kersey*
b. 1856
d. 1950

Sarah E.
b. Unknown
d. Unknown

*James H.
Kersey*
b. 1859
d. 1920

*Mary Ann
Emanuel*
b. 1861
d. 1947

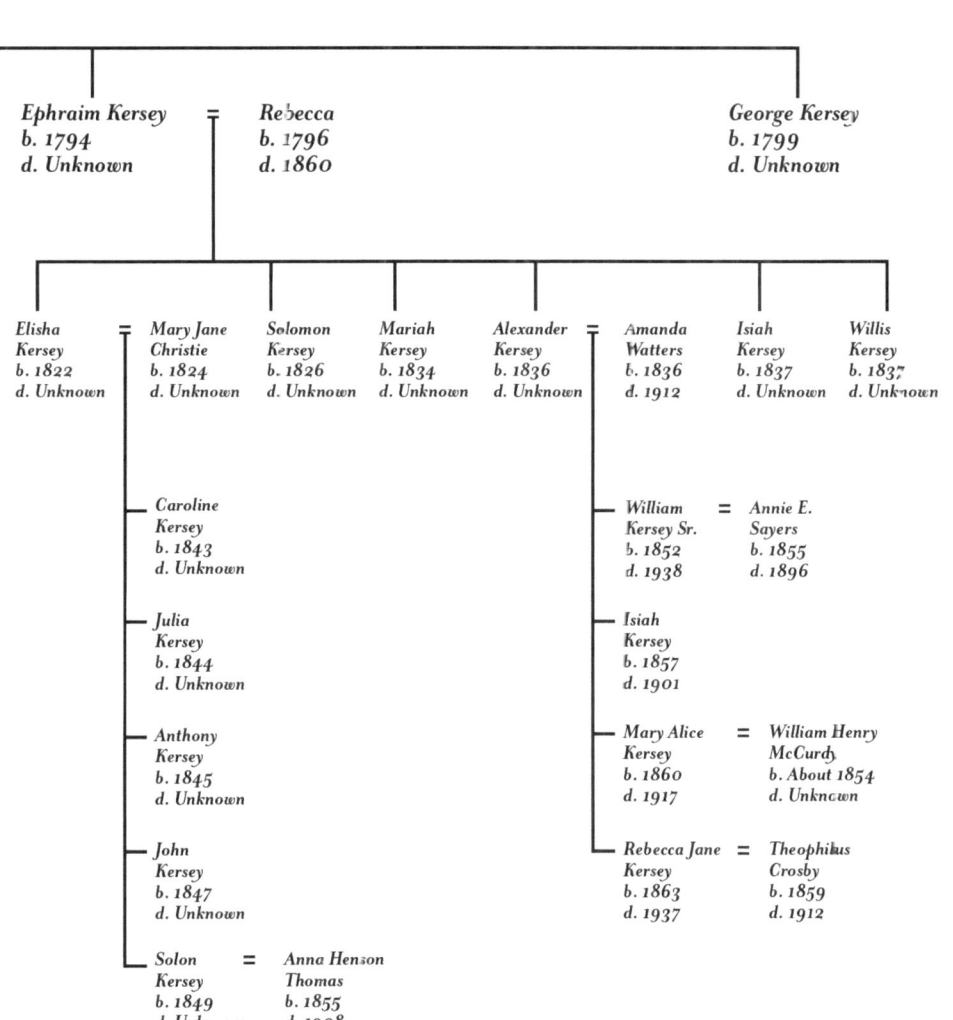

Ephraim Kersey
b. 1794
d. Unknown

=

Rebecca
b. 1796
d. 1860

George Kersey
b. 1799
d. Unknown

Elisha
Kersey
b. 1822
d. Unknown

=

Mary Jane
Christie
b. 1824
d. Unknown

Solomon
Kersey
b. 1826
d. Unknown

Mariah
Kersey
b. 1834
d. Unknown

Alexander
Kersey
b. 1836
d. Unknown

=

Amanda
Watters
b. 1836
d. 1912

Isiah
Kersey
b. 1837
d. Unknown

Willis
Kersey
b. 1837
d. Unknown

Caroline
Kersey
b. 1843
d. Unknown

William
Kersey Sr.
b. 1852
d. 1938

=

Annie E.
Sayers
b. 1855
d. 1896

Julia
Kersey
b. 1844
d. Unknown

Isiah
Kersey
b. 1857
d. 1901

Anthony
Kersey
b. 1845
d. Unknown

Mary Alice
Kersey
b. 1860
d. 1917

=

William Henry
McCurdy
b. About 1854
d. Unknown

John
Kersey
b. 1847
d. Unknown

Rebecca Jane
Kersey
b. 1863
d. 1937

=

Theophilus
Crosby
b. 1859
d. 1912

Solon
Kersey
b. 1849
d. Unknown

=

Anna Henson
Thomas
b. 1855
d. 1908

Interview with Reverend Terrence Vick and Reverend Theron Kersey

TERRENCE VICK: Hello, I am Reverend Terrence Vick. I currently reside in Ypsilanti, Michigan. I'm happy to be with this project. We're excited for the information that's gathered here today.

JOYCE HUNTER: You're a descendant of?

TERRENCE VICK: I am a descendant of David and Agnes Kersey and, locally, John Kersey here in Washtenaw County. And Solon Kersey's family.

JOYCE HUNTER: Reverend Theron Kersey, would you introduce yourself?

THERON KERSEY: My name is Reverend Theron Kersey, born and raised here in Ypsilanti, born in Ann Arbor. I'm connected to David and Agnes Kersey in North Carolina in the 1700s. I'm also originally connected to my great-grandfather John Kersey, who was here in Ypsilanti.

JOYCE HUNTER: Thank you both. The first question is: can you describe your family tree and ancestry?

THERON KERSEY: Well, we started out with ancestry going back to, actually, the earliest part of the 1700s with David and Agnes Kersey. Terry can jump in. It's Ephraim, I believe, was the son of David and Agnes, which comes down to Elisha, who is a Kersey, and then we can go on, and he had six children, one had to be John Kersey. Then after that, my grandfather is Theron Kersey, and my father is Theron Kersey Jr., and I'm Theron Kersey, period. I have six children; Pamela Olds, Patricia Lewis, Margaret Miles, Julia Gilbert, Jennifer Jenkins, and Kristin, she just got married, I can't remember her name now, but we'll just put Sutton there [LAUGHTER], and my son Theron Kersey IV. Those are my children. Each of my seven children had children, which makes me the grandfather of those children. Pamela Olds had Asia and Ariana; Patty had nine; Anthony, Patricia. You're really picking my brain out. We got: Janiston and then Theron, and then we go down to Christina, John, Olivia, Brian, and Demetria. Then next up is Margaret, she had two sons: Caleb, Preston; and then after her is Julie had two children, Jamii Junior and Jordan Gilbert. After her comes Jennifer, Shanice Brewer and Jacqueline and Emanuel Jenkins. After her comes Janiston: had two children, Javon Wilson and Navea Thomas. Of course, my son doesn't have any children.

JOYCE HUNTER: Okay. Thank you. You did it. [LAUGHTER] Terrence, did you want to add to this question?

TERRENCE VICK: Yes. We're stemming from the John Kersey line and very interesting facts on him. Prior to coming to Washtenaw County and Ypsilanti, the family came, he was born in Noblesville, Indiana, and then he came from Noblesville, which is north of Indianapolis, into Canada—Dresden, Canada. And the interesting saga is that they were considered, in some portions of the lineage, as Indian and mulatto. However, Kersey stems from Elisha, as cousin Bill said, and these ancestors were very talented, they had carpentry skills and farming, they lived on farms and the story that we know of them prior to coming into Ypsilanti, they lived in Dresden, and they had the rearing of Reverend Josiah Henson, which is the *Uncle Tom's Cabin*, Harriet Beecher Stowe, her novel. Our family was a part of the living history and saga. The Kerseys joined into the Hensons, and this gives us a rich family dynamic prior to John Kersey family coming into Ypsilanti.

JOYCE HUNTER: Okay. Thank you. You started to answer a little bit of this, but the second question is: when did your family arrive in the Ann Arbor / Ypsilanti / Washtenaw County area? You might have shared a little bit already, but you can add to it.

TERRENCE VICK: We have strong suspicions that the Kersey families were conductors themselves of the Underground Railroad. And this is how it begins. In 1850, the Fugitive Slave Act was enforced. The John Kersey, the Elisha Kersey clan had to flee from Indiana through the Underground Railroad, they came through Kalamazoo, Battle Creek, to Ypsilanti, Detroit, and into Colchester.

TERRENCE VICK: However, some of the children stayed in the Battle Creek–Kalamazoo area. We find them on the 1860 census in Kalamazoo. Then going on into Colchester and to Dresden, but coming into Washtenaw County, they've left those farms, and Ypsilanti had a booming enterprise of several kinds of businesses. For instance, lumber—I even heard someone had an underwear business. But we find John living around 1880 on William Cornwell's enterprise. Just Factory Street where the Ford plant was below Chidester Street, going into the Huron River in Ypsilanti. We had him there, and then his family grew up in Ypsilanti. I believe his first wife passed, and then he later marries Jenny Sparks in Washtenaw County around 1892, and then Bill's great-grandfather, grandfather Theron Kersey I, was born, from the second union right here in Ypsilanti, Washtenaw County, in 1892. But John had an interest from leaving the farm into, I believe, the enterprises that attracted Black families to the Washtenaw county area from various points. But this is where John came into Ypsilanti around 1880.

JOYCE HUNTER: So we're going to go on to question three. Were there any local places of importance for your family? If so, please describe the place and why it was important to your ancestors.

THERON KERSEY: Is that in Ypsilanti?

JOYCE HUNTER: Yes.

THERON KERSEY: One was Brown Chapel. My grandfather was minister of music for 40 years at Brown Chapel. The old Brown Chapel. There is many of them that are buried—family members that we're talking about—are buried in Highland Cemetery, and some are buried at Auburn Cemetery out in the country off of Bemis Road. Those are, and some of them might be buried off of Stoney Creek. Behind used to be the old Methodist church on Stoney Creek Road. Then those are points of interest. There are others that are buried at United Memorial Cemetery in Superior Township.

JOYCE HUNTER: Thank you. If we go to question four, are there any people, artifacts, or pictures unique to your family that you would like to share?

TERRENCE VICK: Well, I'll start with the photo of myself and Reverend Kersey and my cousin. We had a keen interest in our family history. We didn't know how extensive it was until we started collaborating—I think about thirteen years ago, if that—and just digging, and I'm thankful for county archives and local archives that house information concerning family history. That's of utmost importance these days. Because not only ancestry, but it's important going into the museums, looking at family histories written and comparing, and of course, in the African-American community, oral tradition is strong. However, you need back up, you need research, so I'm thankful for the African-American Washtenaw County and the Ann Arbor District Library for bringing this information together. And I'm almost forgetting the question—is anything of importance in our family exhibit? Bill and myself, we were interviewed by the Ypsilanti Historical Library on Huron Street. This was important because, when we initially started, a lot of our history was not available. I felt that there was a resurgence and interest for the Black history to be insured and to be recorded and to be archived for so many people that don't have a notable history of their family. So, I do believe for myself and Bill, we were on Huron Street at the Ypsilanti Historical Society taking a picture as you see in the exhibit there.

JOYCE HUNTER: Right, and I recall that you've already included that, I think, in the dropbox that we provided?

TERRENCE VICK: My cousin gave you the article that was featured in the Ypsilanti history.

JOYCE HUNTER: I do have that, and we'll have to get it into the dropbox as well.

TERRENCE VICK: Okay.

JOYCE HUNTER: Okay. So, Reverend Kersey, do you want to add to that question? You want me to repeat it?

THERON KERSEY: No. I think Terry covered most of it, just most of the pictures. I think we did an article at the Ypsilanti Historical Museum, I know I think I sent you a copy of it, that gives some history of our family. Because there was a lot of that Terry had put in and a number of families that were involved, and that's also there. When you say "pictures," I would love to have pictures of John. I do have a picture of Jenny, who was John's second wife. Her maiden name was Sparks. That was Theron and Augusta's mother. I do have that picture. There's other pictures that I have of my father and Terry's father. We do have that picture, and then there's actually—if you look in the magazine, you have a picture of my grandfather, Theron.

JOYCE HUNTER: So thank you. Those are our four questions.

Elisha Kersey

Julia Kersey

Anthony Kersey

Jenny Kersey

Bill & Theron Kersey

Theron Kersey

Olive Kersey

Solon Kersey's Sons

Solon Kersey's Daughters

Rev. Theron & Rev. Terrence Vick

A Memorial to be registered pursuant to the Statute in such case made and provided, of an Indenture Tripartite made the Thirtieth day of November in the Year of our Lord One thousand eight hundred and Sixty. in pursuance of the Act to facilitate the Conveyance of Real Property. By and Between Ephraim Kersey of the Township of Colchester in the County of Essex and Province of Canada, Yeoman. of the First Part. Elizabeth Kersey of the same place. Wife of the said party of the first part of the Second Part. and Susan Jane Hope also of the same place Widow of the Third Part.

Whereby the said party of the first part. for and in consideration of the Sum of Ten Dollars of lawful Money of the Province of Canada, to him in hand paid by the said party of the third part, the receipt whereof is acknowledged. Did give, grant, bargain, sell, alien, release, convey and confirm unto the said party of the third part his heirs and assigns forever, All that certain parcel or tract of land and premises, situate lying and being in the Township of Colchester in the County of Essex and Province of Canada aforesaid containing by admeasurement Seven Eighteenths of an acre be the same more or less, being composed of par-

1860 Colchester Farm Deed

part of the North half of Lot number Eight in the Fourth of Concession of the said Township of Colchester, which said Seven Eighteenths of an acre of land is therein described as follows. That is to say Commencing at the distance of Six Chains Twelve links South from the North East Angle of said lot number Eight on the limits between said lot and lot number Nine. Thence South upon said limits Two chains eight links more or less to a stake planted for a boundary, then West Two Chains eight links more or less to a stake planted for a boundary, thence North Two chains eight links more or less to a stake planted for a boundary, thence East Two chains eight links more or less to the place of beginning. To have and to hold unto the said party of the Third Part her heirs and assigns to and for her and their sole and only use forever, And by the same Indenture it is Witnessed that the said party of the Second Part, Wife of the said party of the first part hath thereby barred her Dower in the said lands,

Which said Indenture is Witnessed by William Campbell of the Township of Colchester and Matthew Matthews of the same place. And this

1860 Colchester Farm Deed

this Memorial thereof is hereby required to be
registered by me, the said Grantor therein named
                    Witness my hand and Seal at Col-
=chester this thirtieth day of November One thousand
eight hundred and Sixty.
Signed and Sealed
in the Presence of   Susan Jane   her X   Hope
                                            mark

William Campbell
Matthew Mathews

Canada   William Campbell of the
County of Essex   Township of Colchester in the
    To Wit   County of Essey in the Province of
                  Canada - Yeoman, in the annexed
Memorial named, maketh Oath and Saith
that he was present and did see the Indenture
to which said Memorial relates, duly executed
signed, Sealed and delivered by therein named
parties Ephraim Kersey and Elizabeth
Kersey respectively, and that he is a subscribing
Witness to the Execution of the said Indenture
        And further, that he this Deponent
also saw the said Memorial duly signed and
sealed by the therein named Susan Jane Hope
                                            for

1860 Colchester Farm Deed

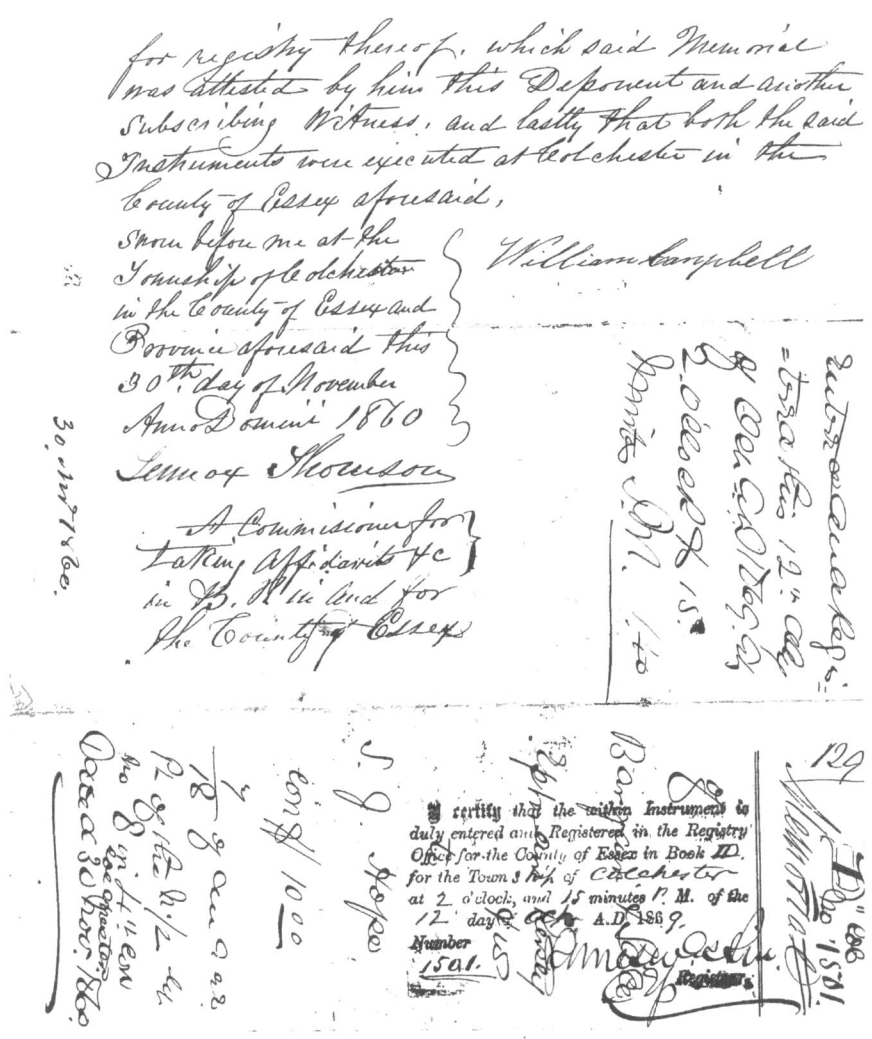

1860 Colchester Farm Deed

Ypsilanti
GLEANINGS
Official publication of the Ypsilanti Historical Society, featuring articles and reminiscences of
the people and places in the Ypsilanti area

Georgia, Indiana, Canada, and Finally Ypsilanti

BY PASTOR THERON W. "BILL" KERSEY III

Julia Lawson-Kersey
(Grand Daughter of Josiah Henson)

Ypsilanti Gleanings, *Summer 2022*[17], *Ypsilanti Historical Society*

The Life and Ancestry of
Olive Pearl Green
Boland Kersey Evans

BY THERON WILLIAMS KERSEY III AND JUDY JACKSON

Olive Green Evans - After her graduation
from Michigan State Normal College in 19·

Theron William Kersey III (a.k.a. "Brother Bill"), is the retiring pastor of the Community Church of God, 565 Jefferson St. Ypsilanti, Michigan. Pastor Kersey has served not only his church, but the community of Ypsilanti for 56 years. Theron is married to his lovely wife, Geanne, and has seven children: Pamela Oldes, Patricia Lewis, Margaret (Peggy) Miles, Julia Gilbert, Jennifer Jenkins, Janiston Sutton, Theron William Kersey IV. He has twenty-two grandchildren and four great-grandchildren. Theron is a member of The Washtenaw Regional Organizing Coalition (WeROC), the Covenant Pastors Fellowship, and the Council for Pastors. Theron was appointed by then Governor Jennifer Granholm to the Michigan State Prison Re-entry program in Washtenaw County. Theron was the past board director and current board member of Ypsilanti's Hope Clinic and Center (located at 518 Harriet St), which provides medical, dental and social services to Ypsilanti.

Because of his rich ancestry, Pastor Kersey, a history buff himself, wants to share his family stories, demonstrating how African Americans have always been a part of Ypsilanti, contributing to its growth through religion, industry, self-reliance and education. How many know that "Free" Black people lived in Ypsilanti and Washtenaw County before the civil war, and before the United States annexed Michigan in 1837? Black people came to Ypsilanti as settlers from the East and freedom-seekers from the South. Ypsilanti also has strong ties to Black Canadian settlements, especially those settlements in the area of Upper Canada, now known as Ontario. Many of those Canadian settlements were in Kent and Essex counties, such as: Anderdon, Marble Village, Union, Gambia, Haiti Village, Brion, Dawn, Elgin, Dresden, Shrewsbury, Puce, Elmstead, Little River, Gosfield, Gesto, Gilgal, New Canaan, the Matthew Settlement, Edgar, Mt. Pleasant, Rochester, Harrow, and the Refugee Home Society Settlement.

Pastor Kersey's first contribution to YHS Gleanings publication is to introduce you to his grandmother, who was born Olive Pearl Green, but many who attended Harriet/Perry School in the 1940s, and 1950s remember her as Mrs. Evans. We cannot talk to you about Olive unless we talk about her family history.

Olive Pearl was the child of Arthur Green and Nellie Jane McCurdy who were married in 1892 in Colchester, Canada. Olive Pearl was the youngest of five children. The Green family emigrated from Canada to the United States in 1903, when Olive was just a toddler. The family lived at 423 South Adams St. here in Ypsilanti.

The Pearl Family: Arthur Green's family had connections with Ypsilanti prior to their 1903 arrival. Arthur's maternal grandparents were Bazel (Basil) Pearl and Catherine Hilton Pearl. Census records report that some of Bazel's children lived in Ypsilanti and surrounding townships as early as 1879. The 1820 US Census reports that Bazel lived in Green County, Pennsylvania as a free man of color. The Pearls were a mixed-race family that moved westward from Pennsylvania because of the changing laws regarding interracial marriages. Bazel Pearl is listed as a resident of Ypsilanti and died in Ypsilanti prior to 1871. The Pearl family also appeared to move back and forth from Michigan to Canada, depending on the political climate and the availability of work. Bazel and Catherine's eighth child was Nancy Ann Pearl, who married Gilbert Green on March 13, 1868, in Essex, Ontario, Canada, and who became parents to Arthur Green and grandparents to Olive Pearl Green.

John Green, formerly known as Elisha Young.

The Green Family: Arthur Green's paternal ancestry can be traced back to John Green, born in 1809. He was the son of a slave owner, Peyton Young of Virginia. John Green, formerly known as Elisha (Young) was born in either Kentucky or Virginia according to contradicting records. Family history says that Elisha married Charlotte Brown in 1828 in Mason County, KY. Charlotte lived on a neighboring plantation. From that union, three children were born: Gabriel Amos (1834), Candes (1835) and Polly Ann (1838). In 1837, Elisha, who had been ill, discovered that his master planned to sell him 'down river" to the Deep South. After a

Ypsilanti Gleanings, Winter 2021[18], Ypsilanti Historical Society

Afterword

*Family Foundations: Four Stories of Black Washtenaw County
Community Building 1850 to 1950*

Claire Zimmerman

IN THE FALL OF 2019, Mike Steinberg asked me to join an advisory
board to explore racially restrictive covenants on housing deeds in
Washtenaw County. These covenants still existed, and Mike wanted to
know what to do about them. Should they simply be removed without
comment? Or did they provide an opportunity to create public aware-
ness about the history of racial prejudice right where people lived?
Delayed by the pandemic, Mike's effort didn't get fully underway until
May 2020. Events of May 25 of that year made the project newly urgent.
The death of George Floyd underscored what many already knew: that
racism was alive and well in the U.S., and that to fight it openly and
ubiquitously with all the tools that could be brought to bear upon it was
the obligation of all.

As a member of the Education subcommittee of the subsequently
baptised *Justice InDeed*, I had met its Chair, Joyce Hunter, at early Advisory Board meetings. As the Education committee got going, it became
immediately clear that Joyce knew how to run a meeting with expertise
and efficiency—better than anyone I can recall in a thirty-year career.
We reported out, we created new assignments for our members, and we

nearly always finished on time or early, no matter how much we had to discuss. As Mike's effort grew and expanded into a community engagement project initiated by Matthew Countryman, Joyce's participation became as central as it was invaluable to all parts of the *Black Washtenaw County* project.

My responsibility in *Black Washtenaw County* was to organize a group on Race in Arts and the Built Environment (RABE) and to serve as PI for the second year of our generous U-M grant. Interested graduate students and I attended events and studied the arts communities of Washtenaw County, seeking a project that would relate meaningfully to the overall *BWC* mission. We struggled to find "a way in" to the project; we had some ideas, but nothing had taken concrete form; we were struggling with our lack of knowledge of local community history. One day, Joyce asked to join our meeting, where she laid out the first sketch for *Family Foundations*. Thus, in one stroke, she gave our group a *raison d'etre*. We were as delighted as we were grateful, and from that point forward, work on this project proceeded.

It is to Joyce that we owe this book and the exhibition that it commemorates. Yet it is not only her personal efforts that brought it into being but also her ability to organize, inspire, and direct many other people. The research that went into its curation is all new research, conducted over the past year or more through painstaking work in the Bentley archives—where U-M archivist Brian Williams has assisted expertly—and from local news outlets, public libraries, and historical societies in the county. Joyce also pursued the contributions of descendants of the original four families for testimonies, adding their personal recollections and family lore to the other evidence that had been amassed. All of this work took time and considerable effort once the original conception had been arrived at—two families from Ann Arbor, two from Ypsilanti, traced back to the mid-nineteenth century.

It has been especially interesting and rewarding to see Joyce working closely with graduate students in the History of Art and Architecture at Michigan, students who never expected to work with the local community when they arrived in Ann Arbor from South Korea, Germany, or Egypt. Yet each of them has enlisted in Joyce's corps, eager to help bring her vision of *Family Foundations* to fruition. It is to be hoped that they will carry the lessons learned into their future lives so that local community building comes to be seen as part and parcel of membership in any academic community. Soyoon Ryu, who has been a member of the team since the beginning, left Ann Arbor for Seoul in May of 2022. Despite the time zone difference, despite the distance, she and Joyce continued to work together on exhibition- and book-related materials. Sometimes Soyoon joined us for meetings at 2:00 am Seoul time.

Among other rewarding aspects of this project was the remarkable Story Map[19] that Mostafa Salama of the Taubman College of Architecture and Urban Planning created with Joyce's input and assistance. The Story Map seeks to connect the history of Black experience in Washtenaw County with the places where it happened. This is the architect's and urban historian's contribution: let's localize history on the streets where it unfolded; by doing so, let's try to see how architecture and urbanism relate to social relations. The only way to do this is to research and recreate the conditions of the past using graphic and visual tools.

We have had other dedicated collaborators from the students of Michigan, many of whom have developed their own relationship with Joyce and our other community partners. Mia Glionna was our lead web designer, creating no less than two websites for our use, but she was also a member of the Exhibition subcommittee of BWC, and she and Joyce have worked closely together over two years. Similarly, Bailey Sullivan and Charlene Hobbs have provided their expertise for BWC; Bailey while studying medieval German architecture; Charlene while working full-time for an architectural firm in Seattle, phoning in early to join our meetings. We relied on the work of Jack Schmitt, Mostafa, and Meghana Tummala (in Mexico City for a fellowship) to guide Family Foundations and the BWC website after the conclusion of the U-M grant.

This, to my mind, has been a deeply rewarding version of engaged local community-and-university work. When community members lead, the university can follow with its lumbering gait, its over-stuffed saddle bags, its byzantine rules and restrictions—and its abundant supply of young talent. Professors oil the machinery and connect the wires so that cogs and signals can move where they need to go. Community members, when they work like Joyce, and students like those we had in BWC work together to create magical outcomes. These two groups—the students and the community partners—tell the institution what to do, not the other way around. Big research universities expect their faculty to play leading roles in ground-breaking research and to translate that leadership into action. Working with this team, the first lesson I learned was that it was not my place to lead. I needed, rather, to listen and then facilitate—to troubleshoot for Joyce and her team so that they could realize the vision they collectively created.

Notes

1   https://www.aachm.org/

2   See, for example, https://twitter.com/eji_org/status/1326163896802168832

3   blackwashtenawcounty.org/

4   For more on the African-American History of the North-Central neighborhood, see the AACHM Living Oral History Walking Tour on the website of the Ann Arbor District Library, aadl.org/AACHMwalkingtour

5   Michigan Civil Rights Commission, "Significant Michigan Civil Rights Case Decisions Through 2003," 1-2, www.michigan.gov/-/media/Project/Websites/mdcr/mcrc/significant-decisions.pdf

6   On sundown towns in southeast Michigan, see David M.P. Freund, Colored Property: State Policy and White Racial Politics in Suburban America, (2010).

7   southadamstreet1900.wordpress.com/

8   www.justiceindeedmi.org/mapping

9   mappingprejudice.umn.edu/

10   www.justiceindeedmi.org/mapping

11   To view the HOLC redlining maps, go to dsl.richmond.edu/panorama/redlining

12   Stevens, Stephanie, *Outcast* (Whitehouse Station, New Jersey: Merck & Co., 2003)

13   Mull, Carol E., *The Underground Railroad in Michigan* (Jefferson, North Carolina: McFarland & Company, Inc, 2010)

14   Mull, *UGRR in Michigan*

15   Edward M. Preston, *Captain Roswell Preston of Hampton, Connecticut* (Nevada City, California: Edward M. Preston, 1899)

16   Mull, *UGRR in Michigan*

17   https://ypsihistory.org/wp-content/uploads/2022/09/Ypsilanti-Gleanings-2022.2-Summer.pdf

18   https://ypsihistory.org/wp-content/uploads/2022/01/2021-winter-Gleanings.pdf

19   www.blackwashtenawcounty.org/exhibit/storymap

Image Credits

www.ingramcontent.com/pod-product-compliance
Lightning Source LLC
Chambersburg PA
CBHW040904120626
46551CB00006B/633